Glimpses of Grace

Encouragement for Life's Journey

Sidney Draayer

Project Philip Ministries

Glimpses of Grace © 2012 by Sidney Draayer

Published by
Project Philip Ministries
4180 44th SE
Grand Rapids, MI 49512
www.projectphilipministries.org

ISBN 987-0-9884202-0-5

First Printing, 2012

Cover design by Michael Lautenbach

Dedication

To our son, Ken, who passed away at age 45.
He knew God's grace.
His last words were, "in Christ."

Dr. Sidney Draayer is an ordained minister in the Christian Reformed Church. He served four churches as a pastor for the first 20 years of his ministry and then served as Director of the Christian Counseling Center in Grand Rapids Michigan for thirteen years. For the next fifteen years he directed Paraklesis Ministries, a ministry of encouragement, teaching, and counseling for pastors, spouses, and churches. This book is a compilation of monthly letters he sent to encourage individuals in ministry.

Along Side Of

I would like to introduce you to the purpose of _Glimpses of Grace._ Perhaps I can best do so by telling you about David and Nathan. No, not the Biblical David and Nathan.

David and Nathan are our grandsons. David is the older of the two. He's energetic, athletic, smart (sounds like a grandpa bragging, doesn't it?) and tough. By that I mean he doesn't cry easily. His pain threshold is high, near the top of the chart. Nathan, who is two years younger, is all of the above, but he's more <u>tender</u>. He's by no means a crybaby, but it's easier to tell when he's hurting.

When Nathan was ready to enter kindergarten he had to have some blood drawn at the lab as a follow-up to his pre-school physical. (Everything turned out well). Obviously he didn't like the idea. The day he was scheduled to go he was quiet and even whimpered a little. At that time I was having blood drawn quite frequently so I offered to go with him and his dad as a means of support. He readily accepted. The Saturday morning we left for the lab something happened I will never forget. "Hey, Nate," called David as we were leaving the house, "**I wish I could go for you!**"

"I wish I could go for you." They were words of brotherly love . . . empathy . . . caring . . . sensitivity . . . and encouragement.

I'm sure we all have moments like that . . . moments when we wish we could reach over and remove a burden from someone's shoulders. We'd even carry it ourselves for a while if we could. But, of course, we can't. Yet there is something we can do. We can stand alongside of them and through our presence, our words, and our deeds let them know we care.

That is the purpose of _Glimpses of Grace- Encouragement for Life's Journey._ It is one way of being alongside of you in your daily routine. We all have times in our lives of great elation and fulfillment. Everything is going the way we like it to go. We also have times when we get discouraged. No one seems to care or notice what we are doing. For times like that, these vignettes are a way of offering you an encouraging word. It is a way of saying that in the ups and downs of life we can see a pattern of how God cares for us if we just look a little further.

The wonderful part of the Christian faith is that we trust someone who not only **wished** he could "go for us," but who actually did. By his birth, his life, his resurrection, his ascension and the promise of his coming again his promise rings true when he said, *"Surely I am with you always, to the very end of the age."* (Matthew 28:20b).

Perfection

As home owners Gladys and I have enjoyed the continual task of remodeling and redecorating it. I do the remodeling if it isn't too difficult and we hire the rest out. The redecorating we do together. We split it 50/50 – she decides what needs to be done; I implement her decisions.

When we paint a room, for example, she chooses the color. Then I do my 50%. I move and cover the furniture, do some scraping and sanding, and patch up holes. I get the brushes and rollers ready and do some priming. Then comes the main task – first cutting in and then finishing the job. Afterward I clean up and replace the furniture. We're both happy with our division of labor and agree it's been one of the ways we have bonded in our marriage.

When we painted the living room a few years ago there was an interesting twist. Gladys had a certain tone of blue she wanted. The clerk at the paint store tinted the paint and suggested we put a swatch on the wall. If it was not what she wanted she could return it and he would keep trying until it was right. Well, it wasn't right the first time so we tried again. It was still not quite right. Here our memories clash a little. Gladys says we went back to the store three more times. I say it was five. Let's leave it at quite a few.

When we applied a strip for the 5th time (I still say 7th) Gladys stepped back and said, "That's perfect!" I knew what she meant. What she had in mind was exactly what was on the wall. The color she pictured was now reality. (I must say I like her choice.)

The Christian life is like our experience with paint. We are in the process of becoming perfect. In James 1:4 (KJV) we read, *"But let patience have her perfect work that ye may be _perfect_ (mature – NIV) and entire, wanting nothing."* The word refers to God's desire that we become what he has in mind for us. He is continually shaping us so that we reach the full potential he desires for us. God's mental picture is becoming reality.

Much of the shaping process takes place in the ordinary experiences of life. As we make choices . . . as we interact with people . . . as we do our work . . . as we go through happy times . . . and as we go through difficult times God is molding us into the image of Jesus.

How good it is to know that God is in all that happens to us and in all we do. He is concerned not only what he can do <u>through</u> us, but also what he does <u>in</u> us. We may wonder <u>how</u> we get out of a painful situation. God cares just as much about <u>what</u> we get out of it. What a blessing to know that as we travel the road of life he is leading us to perfection. We can hold to the promise that *"by one sacrifice he (Christ) has made perfect forever those who are being made holy."* (Hebrews 10:14)

Letting Go

Being a native Michiganian I have always enjoyed our many lakes and streams. Nothing is more relaxing than sitting on the beach at Lake Michigan on a hot summer evening feeling the cool breezes and listening to gentle tapping of the waves on the shore.

While I have enjoyed the water, I have not always enjoyed being **in** the water. My innate fear of water was reinforced by my mother who dreaded any kind of submerging in water except our weekly bath. For the first 3 decades of my life I watched my friends and family enjoy swimming and diving while I frolicked in water chest high. Ugh!

My embarrassment grew more acute as our children grew and demonstrated adroitness in their aquatic endeavors. After hearing "It's easy" and "Just do it this way" scores of time my shame was too great. With their coaching I learned to swim well enough so I could enjoy my time in the water with them. Still a little fearful, but I was able to get around.

My confidence increased when a friend showed me how to dive off the edge of a pool. I was elated. Only piloting a 747 plane would have brought me greater joy.

Alas, my ecstasy was short lived. On my fourth or fifth dive I sank to the bottom like a 300-pound person on a cheap motel mattress. Panic! For what seemed like a year I flailed my arms and kicked my feet. All to no avail. It seemed like a giant sea monster was holding me down. I gasped for air, but ingested water instead. "This is what it's like to drown," I told myself. I was frantic. What an ignominious way to end it all. I imagined newspaper headlines. "Young Pastor Ends Career in Big Splash." "Non-Baptist Pastor Fatally Immersed." I decided to stop fighting and prepare for the inevitable. But wait! . . . a miracle . . . I floated to the top. Letting go and relaxing was all I needed to do. (My friend told me later he was ready to jump in when I bobbed to the surface.)

I have been in similar situations – not struggling with water, but with some issue or problem. I am sure you have too. There are times when there seems to be no way out – a severe illness . . . . loss of a friendship . . . a hard decision . . . unjust criticism. We struggle . . . and pray . . . and work. But inner peace is elusive. And then, through the Holy Spirit's nudging, we give it all over to God. We surrender. There is nothing more we can do. And God is there! *"You will cry for help, and he will say, 'Here I am."* we are assured in Isaiah 58:9. As we place ourselves in his hands he supplies our needs.

With Confidence

On our three-week, self-guided tour through Europe in 1989 Gladys and I learned a lesson in communication. We were staying overnight in a picturesque, mountain village in French speaking Switzerland. We ran into a major snag when it came time to eat.

After we were seated in the hotel's outdoor cafe we realized that neither of us recognized a single French word on the menu. I tried to recall some Latin from high school and college. Maybe I'd find a connection. Alas, those cells were inactive.

I knew how to avoid snails, but I envisioned ordering something like sautéed earthworms or rum-soaked pig brains or, worse, fruitcake. I scanned each item laboriously. I had a hunch I knew the French word for fish. When the waitress came for our order I pointed to the word, and asked with exact enunciation: "Fish?" She responded with a blank stare. I repeated my question more slowly, with faultless elocution. Her answer passed me like a 100 mph fastball. Maybe I needed to speak louder. "Fish?" I shouted. She hurled some loud babble back at me.

A few other waitresses saw our plight and tried to help. We tried a few charades, but it only left us all laughing. I tried another tack. "Spreken sie deutsch?" I inquired. Like a genie summoned from a bottle one lady began speaking immaculate German. My feeble German was an enigma to her. A few more people joined the hilarity trying to assist the hapless Americans. Finally one man nodded that it was indeed fish. With a sigh of relief we ordered and enjoyed a great meal.

Our prayer life can have communication snags at times. Our prayers can be thoughtless . . . rote . . . hurried. Our words may be mumbled. How can God accept them and understand? Surely there is a barrier there. But the Holy Spirit is our interpreter. He takes our prayers . . . those we cry out in the throes of pain . . . the prayers we pray on the run . . . the rote petitions offered while our minds roam aimlessly . . . the pleas we utter thinking they probably won't be heard anyway . . . and sanctifies and purifies and presents them to God in perfect form. He shapes them *"in accordance with God's will"* (Romans 8:26).

That is our assurance as we pray. Even in our weaknesses and failures we can come into his presence *"with confidence"* *Hebrews 4:16* and know we are heard.

Perspective

Did you ever have one of those days when everything seems to go wrong? While reminiscing with our daughter Jan recently we laughed about such a day from the past.

It was a scorching July day on our visit to Gil and Jan in Alabama. Gil was on call over night at the hospital so Jan suggested we take the children, Kellie, age 6, and Michael, age 4, camping at Gulf Shores. As veteran campers we readily agreed. Anything for a cool breeze.

We set up two tents and then enjoyed the amenities of camping . . . a stroll on the beach . . . a favorite ice cream cone . . . fun on the playground . . . and then a late night snack. At 10 pm we turned in - Michael and I in one tent; Jan, Gladys and Kellie in the other.

Then . . . disaster! About 2 a.m. a storm blew in . . . rain . . . thunder . . . lightening . . . wind. The works. Puddles formed on the hard Alabama clay and silently crept into the tents. After being awake for almost two hours I decided to sit in the car for a few minutes of respite. Michael was sleeping soundly. The others were quiet. I climbed into my dry haven . . . and then I fell asleep.

At 6 a.m. I was awakened by a loud, angry banging on the window. I found I had been oblivious to a rain-soaked drama. Michael woke up, looked for me, and then began calling for Jan. Jan heard him but assumed I was with him. He was too frightened to find his way out of his watery prison. At long last Jan went to his rescue and took him into their tent, by now a soggy mess. They finally decided the culprit had slept long enough and woke me up. Bah! Embarrassing!

We packed our mucky belongings in the back of Gil's Z-28 and I closed the hatchback. More misfortune. A tent pole got in the way and the hydraulic closing mechanism allowed no interference. Pop! The $ 1,000 back window shattered into 5,000 pieces. A quiet, somber five-some made their way back home in the gentle rain and began the process of repairing and healing.

Although Michael says he still owes me one, we could laugh as we reviewed the misfortunes of that day. We had perspective . . . the bigger picture. On the total screen of life it was just a blip.

We all have "bad" days. God gives us the perspective to see that many were not so bad after all. We deal with them and then forget about them. God gives us the grace to see the truly painful ones against the backdrop of his promise that pain doesn't have the last word. *"Our present sufferings are not worth comparing with the glory that will be revealed in us."* (Romans 8: 18).

Wisdom

Our family tradition is opening our Christmas gifts with a roaring fire in the fireplace. The crackling flame, the fragrant aroma, and the gentle heat all make for a homey atmosphere. As I lit the fire this Christmas I thought about a mishap a few years back.

On a brisk fall day Gladys was running some errands and I decided it would be nice to spend some time in front of the fire when she got home. I skillfully arranged the kindling and logs and put a match to the pile. Then I moved on to the kitchen to make some coffee.

Smoke was billowing into the living room when I returned. A quick diagnosis revealed that I had forgotten to open the damper. The smoke was finding an alternative means of egress. A quick jab with the poker opened the damper thus enabling the smoke to follow its intended path. Meanwhile the nefarious cloud filled the room and was wending its way down the hall.

What to do? In a stroke of genius (panic, really) I turned on the ceiling exhaust fan in the hallway. If it could draw hot air out of the house, why not smoke? Big time mistake! Major league fiasco! The downdraft from the chimney only brought more smoke into the room at a faster pace.

Recovering my sanity, I shut off the fan and opened all the windows and doors. By the time Gladys returned the house was cool, but the thick haze had pretty well disappeared.

How could I make such a blunder? It wasn't a lack of knowledge. I'm familiar with fireplaces and air currents and dampers. I aced physics and chemistry in high school and physical science in college. Facts were not the problem. What I didn't do was apply my store of data. I lacked, in this instance, what the Bible calls wisdom. I didn't relate the facts to the situation.

Life often calls for wisdom. Fostering family and friends . . . co-operating with colleagues . . . determining direction . . . figuring finances . . . all require wisdom. Facts are crucial. But more important is the ability to interpret the facts . . . to connect items . . . to integrate information.

At such times wisdom is available. God promises, *"If any of you lacks wisdom, he should ask God . . . and it will be given to him"* James (1:5). Wisdom is a resource we need continually. Thank God the source never runs dry.

Mysteries

Families have secrets and mysteries. Some family secrets should be kept. Sometime family secrets need to be exposed. Family mysteries are just, well, family mysteries.

We have a family mystery that has been floating around since the mid-1960s. This eerie visitor invaded our family one day when Gladys and I went on a brief errand and left the five children at home. A few hours after returning one of us noticed that someone had engraved the word egg on our dresser in the bedroom. Bah! Who did it?

I decided I would find out who did it . . . give a brief reprimand . . . and then try to repair the damage the best I could. My attempt as an amateur sleuth took an interesting turn. I began with a generic question. "Who did it?" I drew nothing but blanks stares and a few shrugs. I decided I needed to get more specific. I asked each of the children individually if he/she were the culprit. All lips were sealed. My occasional questioning over the next few days did not give me the slightest hint as to who the perpetrator was. Even when I promised there would be no punishment for this misdeed their memories failed them.

I decided to dig deeper into my bag of tricks. I asked each of the children to print the word egg on a piece of paper. Alas, my attempt at deciphering handwriting was a failure. I realized that finding the wrongdoer was probably a hopeless task. I decided to drop it. But I never quite let go. About once a decade I would ask if anyone would like to 'fess up. No luck. At a family reunion two years ago I guaranteed complete amnesty. I only needed to have my curiosity satisfied. It wasn't. The mystery remains a mystery.

Life poses many deeper mysteries than an egg escapade. We are often baffled by what we see and experience. Tragic deaths . . . devastating wars . . . debilitating illnesses . . . unjust criticisms leave us groping for answers that never come. But there is no need to despair. God is still in control and he has promised that someday he will make it plain.

The future is also a mystery. We can't pull the curtain aside and see what lies before us. But we can rest in God's promise that he *"will be our guide even to the end." Psalm 48:14.*

Thank God there is a mystery that has been unraveled! We can know *"the mystery of God, namely Christ, in whom are hidden all the treasures of wisdom and knowledge."* (Colossians 2:2). Thank God for his grace and love! And wonder of wonders, God has chosen us, like Paul, *"to proclaim the mystery of Christ,"* (Colossian 4:3), to the world!

Humility

I couldn't believe the resistance I put up to swallowing 6 pills. After all, I had been ingesting little round cylinders daily for four years. But now I drew the line. I reached my limit. This is it!! I finally succumbed, but not without a battle. Let me give you some background.

My drug regimen began in the summer of 1987. I was diagnosed with a rare disease - Wegner's granulomatosis. My body had become allergic to its own blood vessels. Though formerly fatal, it was now treatable, though not curable. Daily medication put the disease in remission and within 8 weeks I was back to working full time.

Four years later the ugly monster raised its head again. The response? A stronger, more toxic drug . . . one that could have unpleasant side effects.

That's when the battle began. I didn't want a stronger, more toxic drug. My head and my heart were at odds. I kicked and screamed emotionally and mentally. For three full days I pouted on the inside and the outside. Finally, after sitting quietly at Lake Michigan for an hour and talking with Gladys, I surrendered. With great reluctance I downed the pills in one gulp. (I had no adverse side effects and lately am on a much less toxic drug).

Why the resistance? The new meds were meant to help. Why the opposition? One word says it: **pride.** Getting sick and taking pills was bad enough. But now, taking far stronger pills reminded me of my own weakness. I had lost control again. Swallowing these pills would be an admission of my own powerlessness. Reason finally prevailed, but it took time.

Isn't that how we sometime respond to God also? He instructs us for our own good, but we don't always listen well. He tells us what is best for us, but we often don't want him to interfere. We fail to get our way, and we question his care for us. Our pride keeps us from obedience. Our stubbornness prevents us from growing and getting closer to him.

Patiently God nudges us. Gradually he breaks down our resistance. Lovingly he reminds us that we can't do it on our own. *"God opposes the proud, but gives grace to the humble"* I Peter 5:5. Then, when we finally give in, we realize we are in the arms of a loving God who desires only that which is best for us. What a blessing to know that he never gives up on us, and that his will for us is our maturity. What a great God we serve!

Friends

I learned a lot about fire and friends a few years ago. Our son-in-law and daughter's house was completely gutted by fire. We talked a lot by phone, and from listening to them I wrote the following as a response a few days after the fire.

Fire . . . a friend turned fiend.

Starting slowly . . . a puff of smoke . . . a fickle flame . . .
    Then, evolving into a destructive monster,
    Breathing destruction and devastation . . .
    Relentlessly devouring valuables and trifles
without discrimination.

Out of control . . . angry . . . and fierce . . .
    Ruining all it touches.
Putrid smell -
    Penetrating the very fiber of all that remains . . .
    Infiltrating the pores of human skin.

Stubbornly it breathes its last . . .

Its monument:
  A mass of soggy, smelly clothes . . .
  Sooty, charred furniture . . .
  Possessions turned to ashes . . .
  Things alive only in memory.

Numbness takes over . . . then anger . . . and sadness.

But fire brings out friends . . .
  Friends who care . . .
    Who sustain . . .
      Who support.

Their arms give a tender embrace . . .
      Their hands provide practical support,
      Their words speak comfort and solace,
      Their ears listen to feelings of rage and
        fear and grief,
      Their eyes see things that need to be done,
      Their feet run urgent errands.

Friends . . .

> *Provide strength and courage by their presence and prayers, Speak volumes through their understanding silence, Take over when appropriate, Retreat when solitude is important.*

Friends . . . Pick up the load

> *Allow expression of emotions . . . Shed a tear, and even, sometime, a laugh.*

Friends . . . a gift from God . . .

> *A gift of love . . . compassion . . . peace . . . and trust.*

Fire empties the heart and leaves an ache.

Friends help temper the ache . . .

> *. . . And fill the heart with love and gratitude.*

All of us have times when life is difficult. Praise God for those friends who stand by us and become God's instruments of grace. Above all, we have "*a friend who sticks closer than a brother.*" (*Proverbs* 18:24).

Pain

It was the best blow I ever struck in my life. I never was much of a fighter. I had the usual childhood scuffles, but few major bouts. But this poke was a masterpiece. Right on target. Smack on the nose. A pro boxer would have been proud to deliver it.

Alas, it was the wrong person . . . at the wrong time . . . for the wrong reason. Here's why.

I always hated long periods between exams. I did better when I took them in quick succession. In my third year of seminary I had a day and a half between two exams. It was torture. It seemed like I was getting a taste of eternity. I had no trouble finding diversions instead of studying. Meanwhile the inner tension gradually rose.

The clock slowly crept to noon on the day of the exam and Gladys and I had a light lunch. Before I left, in my neurotic desire to work off a little nervous energy, I initiated a little horseplay. I put her in a headlock and feigned a couple of jabs to her nose. I had done this before and we generally had a good laugh about it. But

33

now, it misfired. One of my pretend blows caught her flush on the nose. Ouch! Double ouch!

Instant panic! I couldn't take it back. My apologies sounded hollow. The damage had been done. When the shock wore off she assured me she would be all right. Eventually she was, but not before she endured her share of pain. Fortunately, neither her nose nor our relationship suffered permanent damage, though both took time to heal. Even though I had not meant to hit her the pain for her was real . . . undeserved . . . and senseless.

Much of the pain we suffer seems that way too. Pain often barges into our lives as an unwelcome and irrational intruder. Many times it seems to fall on the wrong person. It disrupts our lives . . . strains relationships . . . and causes confusion.

Pain can also, however, be an occasion of healing. God uses it as his tool to correct us when we have strayed. The ache caused by a bad habit . . . a broken relationship . . . an overt or covert sin is his way of calling us to return to him. When we do, he is there!

34

More often God uses pain as a time when he lovingly helps us to grow. *"God disciplines us for our good, that we may share in his holiness.* (Hebrews 12:10). In times of pain we gradually rediscover who he really is . . . how much he truly loves us . . . and that he is always with us. That's our great comfort in pain!

Even as we experience pain . . . some of it severe . . . we live with the blessed promise that someday *"there will be no more pain."* (Revelation). 21:4. Praise God!

Surprises

Coming from Dutch descent, one of my favorite pastries has always been "olie bollen" (oil balls), a.k.a "vet bollen" (fat balls). The names say it all. Making them is fairly simple. Stir the right mixture of flour, sugar and other ingredients (raisins are optional) and roll up into small balls. Drop the balls into hot oil and fry for a few minutes. Rolled in sugar they're great. Healthy? Hardly. Tasty? Hard to beat!

Gladys and I have an "olie bollen" tale we still chuckle about. Dave, an insurance salesman, who began attending one of the churches we served, asked us if he could tell us what he had to offer. We were honestly interested, so we agreed. He arrived early one afternoon to show us his product.

Since he wasn't of Dutch descent Gladys decided to treat Dave to some "olie bollen" along with a cup of coffee. At the appropriate time she served us and we continued talking.

I eagerly bit into the "olie boll". Ugh. Disaster city! The outside was great, but the inside? . . . raw dough. Soup in a shell. The oil hadn't been hot enough. Gladys took her first bite. Oh, no! A red face. How did this ever happen? We tried to eat as nonchalantly as we could, but through our slurping and chewing both of us felt thoroughly embarrassed. What a way to treat a potential church member. We were relieved when Dave licked off his fingers and put his plate down.

Gladys offered him a second cup of coffee. Then . . . the unexpected. "Those banana fritters are really good," he said, "do you mind if I have another?" Yes! Victory snatched from the jaws of defeat. A failure turned into a success . . . embarrassment to pride!

On a deeper level isn't that true of life? God can turn things around when we feel we've messed up. A "plastic smile" is used to bless . . . a word spoken without thought becomes a source of healing . . . a small deed is transformed into a mountain of encouragement . . . a poor decision brings us on the path to better things.

That's the way it is in God's economy. When we place ourselves in his hands he assures us that he can use even our weakness and inadequacies to his praise, to our good, and to the welfare of others. What a great source of encouragement! He always does *"immeasurably more than we ask or think"* (Ephesians 3:20).

God Understands

I came home from school as excited as any fifth grader could be. It was the opportunity of a lifetime! I couldn't wait to tell my parents. A men's service group was sponsoring an outing for all boys in grades 4, 5, and 6. It was a one-day train excursion to Detroit to tour Greenfield Village and the Henry Ford museum. History was my favorite subject so it would be fascinating to view Edison's laboratory and a host of other historical objects. To save money we would take a sack lunch to eat there and be back in Grand Rapids in time for dinner. The cost would be only $2.00.

I can remember how excited I was as I told my parents. What a great day it would be! Lots of great experiences. My first train ride. My first visit there. The camaraderie with classmates. A day off from school! It doesn't get any better than this! My parents shared the excitement, but were hesitant to say all right. A few days later I found out why. They did not have the $2.00. It was the tail end of the great depression. My father hadn't worked for years because of an accident. They simply didn't have the money.

On the day of the great event I was one of only two boys in my class who didn't go. The other one had no interest. I was very disappointed, **but it was o.k.** I wanted to go, but I accepted it. I know why. My parents' 'no' was in the context of love. I knew they loved me. But even more than that, I knew they understood. I remember the pained look on my father's face as he broke the news. I'm sure it hurt them as much as it hurt me. That made the difference. My situation didn't change, but they understood! That's all I needed to know.

Life can be disappointing at times. Not only for children, but also for adults. A dream is shattered . . . a friendship sours . . . people turn on us . . . resources dwindle . . . children go astray . . . there is little appreciation for our efforts. We feel down . . . disappointed . . . alone.

But we're not alone. God understands. He feels our pain. He knows what we're going through. He fathoms the depth of our feelings. He *"has compassion on his children*" (Psalm 103:13). Through his Holy Spirit he assures us that he is mindful of our plight. Sometime he does so through his word. Sometime we know it intuitively. Often people who understand become his messengers of assurance. However he does it, we know he is there. He comprehends. He cares. And finally that is all that matters.

Integrity

Gladys and I meandered down memory lane last summer. We took a tour of Ludington State Park in northern Michigan, the venue of many happy weeks of camping with our family. It was fun to see the various sites where we camped and to recall our children's activities and our family time around the campfire each night.

We didn't become campers by choice. With five children and a pastor's salary we felt it was the only way we could vacation. We bought a tent and all the paraphernalia that goes along with it – sleeping bags, air mattresses, a cooler, a camp stove-the works.

The first week was a near disaster. Water poured into our tent the first night during a thunderstorm. Daily, at least one of the children would be lying on a blanket in the shade of a tree not feeling well. Sand in the food was commonplace. Clean and dirty clothes soon became indistinguishable. After a week Gladys and I were ready to literally pitch our tent . . . and everything else too. But

. . . the kids loved it. They were having a great time. We stayed. Camping became an annual family event for the next 15 years.

I do recall one positive event from that first year. We didn't have enough cash when we went to buy groceries so I asked the manager if I could write him a check. I expected to jump through some hoops since I was from out of state. To my surprise he readily agreed. "Do you need identification?" I asked. His reply has always stayed with me. "In all my years in business I've never had a camper give me a bad check," he said, "It's o.k." Wow! Things have changed in the last 50 years, but to him campers had integrity.

Integrity is at the core of the Christian faith. We serve a God of integrity – one who is truthful . . . reliable . . . and upright. *"God is not a man, that he should lie."* (Numbers 23:19). He always acts on what he says; he always fulfills what he promises.

We are called to reflect his integrity. That means being totally honest in relating to others . . . dropping facades we have in order to look good . . . keeping our promises .

. . valuing truth over success. In a world filled with duplicity that is not always easy. But it is vital if we are to live with a clear conscience and do effective ministry.

Integrity comes only as we cultivate our personal walk with God. Like David we need to say, *"I have set the Lord always before me."* (Psalm 16:8). I urge you to spend enough time in his presence. Then your life and your work will mirror his faithfulness and veracity.

Deception

Gladys and I had an unusual encounter a few years ago in Bucharest, Romania. We decided to take a brisk walk in the warm sunshine to clear the fog from our heads and kinks from our bodies after a long trans-Atlantic flight. While walking down the drive from the hotel to the main street we met a well-dressed young man who asked us in broken English if we knew where a park was. Being a little familiar with the area I pointed him in the right direction. In response to his question whether we were tourists we nodded agreement.

A moment later two other men came up to us, the older one flashing an official looking identification card. I assumed, as did Gladys, they were police. The older man asked if the young man we were talking to was trying to buy or sell drugs. Even after we said no, he persisted in further questioning. He wanted to see my passport. No go. It was in the hotel. He asked to see my money. After some hesitation I took a few Romanian leis ($10 to $12 US) from my pocket. (I had $600 US in another pocket). At his insistence I showed him my wallet which, as always, contained zilch. After a few more exchanges all three left. Whew! Instant relief! We hadn't been detained. We hadn't been busted or arrested! We had done no wrong, but you never know when you're in another country.

When I told our missionary friend who picked us up to take us to the retreat site, he assured us it was a scam. They look at your money, he told us, distract you, give you back some of your money and leave with the rest. English speaking tourists are the most likely targets, although even some long-time missionaries have been bilked.

On reflection the thought kept recurring how easily I believed the shyster. He looked and sounded so official. Even though I lost no money I complied quite easily with most of what he demanded. I knew it was all a little strange, but it seemed real. I believed his lie.

Our world abounds with lies. It's easy to believe them at times. Bigger is better . . . taking time away from my work is sloth . . . if I tell people how I feel, I will be rejected . . . others are always happy and have things together . . . appearance is primary . . . money and material goods bring happiness We believe the world's lies only to our own hurt. They quickly sabotage our effectiveness and our relationships.

How we need to focus on God's truth . . . on what he says about the real basis for our acceptance . . . on taking Sabbath . . . on honesty in relationships . . . on his values . . . and on his provision. Let your daily prayer be: *"guide me in your truth, and teach me."* (Psalm 25:4).

Unique

In our lighter moments some of my children have a not so subtle way of reminding me both of my age and my peculiarities. They'll ask me how they can tell when I've "lost it." How will they know, they wonder, when it's time to give dad "special care?" So I've given them a checklist, which will indicate when dad is probably "over the hill." If they hear only one of the following statements it's only an 'uh-hu.' Hearing two only means 'Watch it! Three signifies 'this is probably it.'

- "I'd do anything right now for a slice of fruitcake."
- "I sure hope Michigan State beats Michigan in football today."
- "It doesn't matter if we're late for the meeting again."
- "It's 10 p.m. I think I'll go to bed."
- "I really don't want to see the grandkids for a while."

- "I'm going to wear over-the-calf black socks with white tennis shoes and shorts."
- "We can clean this mess up later, no rush."
- "Let's wear matching outfits when we go out tonight."
- "Would you add a couple of maraschino cherries to my sundae?"
- "I'm throwing all these maps away."

I've raised a few eyebrows occasionally, but no major blunders yet.

All of us, of course, have characteristics that make us distinct. Like snowflakes, no two of us are alike . . . sometime to our delight; sometime to our chagrin. We vary in personality . . . tastes . . . gifts . . . peculiarities . . . and experiences. God has made each of us unique.

That's great as long as we can accept ourselves. Yet, that's not always easy. We may get down on ourselves because we're not as outgoing . . . or fluent . . . or quick-witted . . . or successful as others. Then we're tempted to work harder in order to validate ourselves. We need to prove we are acceptable. The truth is: enough is never enough.

That's why we need continual reminders of grace. Simply put, God accepts us for who we are. We don't need to impress him or others with our skills or cleverness or hard work. We should strive for excellence, but not to prove anything. *"God knows how we were formed."* (Psalm 103:14) and "God's love for us is *"unfailing"* (Psalm 13:5). Believing that frees us for more effective service as well as greater enjoyment of God's world.

Focus

Thanks to the urging of three grandsons I entered a new world a few years ago - the fast-paced world of racecars. I had the thrill of guiding a ton of sleek steel around a 2-mile track at speeds up to187 miles an hour. Wow!
.

The NASCAR Speedway in a local mall consists of a realistic-looking racetrack with all the action projected on a wall and controlled by computers. Their slogan is, "So real you can feel it." It was an ad that was absolutely true! We each entered a stationary racecar, tightened our seat belts and waited for the countdown. Then the countdown began - three ... two ... one ... go! I timidly stepped on the gas and joined the pack of 17 other cars. The first few laps were just a struggle for survival. Cars zipped by me at warp speed. I fought desperately with my car which was determined to smash into the wall. The track seemed to narrow into a mere footpath. Sweat cascaded from pores I didn't know I had. My arms and legs had the consistency of a bowl of soggy cereal. I rapidly became a believer in temporary insanity.

Finally my 71-year-old competitive instincts kicked in. I began to shed my trepidation. I put "the pedal to the metal," as they say. I started to maneuver the banked turns with the skill of a pro. I felt an adrenaline rush as I picked up speed on the straightaway. I smugly zoomed by a few laggards. Even though I trailed a majority of the other drivers, I crossed the finish line with a feeling of exhilaration.

What I realized later as I reflected on my brief fling with speed is that it had all of my attention. I thought about zilch but keeping the speeding monster on course. Nothing distracted me. I felt only the challenge and excitement of the moment. <u>I was focused!</u>

On a much higher plane, focus on God is crucial in our Christian walk. We need constantly to keep our eyes on what he is doing. We need continually to remember his faithfulness . . . his power . . . his presence. Without realizing it we can drift from the course we have chosen. Fears and frustration can lure us from the right path. Issues of minor significance can distract us. Discouragement can soon bring us to a crashing halt.

When we focus on God and his strength we see the bigger picture. That puts us back on track.

The good news is that though we may lose focus at times, God never loses his focus. He has a plan for this world and he will accomplish what he has set out to do. He *"never slumbers or sleeps"* (Psalm 121:4.) There is even more good news! He never loses his focus on us! *"He does not take his eye off the righteous"* (Job 36:7). In every circumstance we are always in his care. He is truly a God of grace.

Mistakes

Sometime when you think you have it all together you find out that you don't.

In the years that Gladys worked full time we often went out to eat 2 or 3 times a week. To avoid the 'I-don't – care-where-we-eat' game we agreed that we would take turns suggesting a place to eat and we would decide from there. In golfing parlance, we each had about one 'mulligan' a month.

One evening Gladys exercised her option and said she didn't care where we ate. I graciously took the lead and suggested Big Boy. She agreed. Then, in yo-yo fashion, she disagreed. Being a truly sensitive husband I said I would defer and go where she wanted to go. She still wasn't sure what she wanted, but after some solemn pondering she said Big Boy would be all right.

To understand the ironic turn our conversation took you need to know that I am a licensed marriage counselor. I have two degrees with an emphasis in marriage and family. I have counseled hundreds of couples as they traversed the sometime rocky road called marriage. An empathetic and caring response would have been "fine." <u>But</u>, what did I say? "No, I'm not going to Big Boy!"

As you can imagine, the rest of our brief discussion went swiftly downhill. We somehow ended going to Big Boy, where we sat for a while throwing big chunks of silence at each other. I am certain everyone in the restaurant was sneaking glances at us to see how the expert would extricate himself from the mess he created. Finally I asked Gladys if she felt comfortable leaving and trying again. She did. I apologized . . . she forgave . . . we left. . . mended some fences, and enjoyed a great evening together.

What did I learn from that inane incident? <u>One</u>, no matter how much we know or how well we are prepared, we make mistakes. Good intentions . . . education . . . and skills do not preclude inappropriate responses . . . poor choices . . . or regrettable acts. No one ever has it all together.

<u>Two,</u> mistakes can be rectified. God has a knack of putting us back on our feet after we have taken a

tumble. We need to keep a spirit of humility . . . teachableness . . . before him and others.

<u>Three</u>, God uses us despite our blunders. He can still, St. Ignatius reminds us, "strike a straight blow with a crooked stick." How wonderful that we are instruments of his grace and love despite our foibles. God still uses the *"foolish things"* and the *"weak things"* in his service. (I Corinthians 1:27,28).

Fear

As a teenager and for many years later I always enjoyed thrill rides at amusement parks. For years I never met a roller coaster or exhilarating ride I didn't like.

But my halcyon days ended on a Ferris wheel. When a gentle gust of wind caused the car to tip back slightly, my mind went amok. I pictured us being abruptly ejected from the car, plunging awkwardly through the air, and splattering on the ground like raw eggs. I was glad to reach *terra firma*. From then on, pardon the pun, it was a downward spiral.

Certain settings triggered a fear after that. I made the trip up the continental divide in the Rocky Mountains on the floor of the gondola car because I was sure the cable would break. I quickly exited an outside elevator of a hotel in San Diego just before it detached from the building and plunged into the street below. Whoops! It was just a mirage.

My *coup de grace* came about some years later when we visited the famous Sugar Loaf Mountain in Rio de Janeiro, Brazil. The cable car ride to the mountain looked 5 miles long. The cables were just two strands of thread. Only my irrational fear stood between a once-in-a-life-time experience and me. After deep deliberation, despite numb legs and sweaty palms, I finally gave the lady my Visa card . . . took the ride . . . and absorbed a view I still savor. I had gone beyond my fear. Yes! Since then I've enjoyed numerous stunning vistas that I might have missed before.

All of us have fears – some of them healthy. They can keep us from harm or wrong. But some fears hamper us. Fear of failure keeps us from personal growth. Fear of intimacy causes us to build walls. Fear of inadequacy prevents us from working to our full potential. We miss opportunities for helping others for fear of criticism. Fear of the future produces inner turmoil. Fear of rejection puts new experiences out of reach.

That's why we need to hear anew the message of the angels to the shepherds in Bethlehem. *"<u>Do not be afraid</u>. I bring you good news of great joy that will be for all the* *people"* (Luke 2:10). The good news at Christmas is that God is in control and we belong to him. He promises that he will walk with us as we struggle with trepidation and doubts. We can work through our fears because he has overcome them for us. That is cause for rejoicing during this special season and all through the year! He reminds us in his word that *"perfect love drives out all fears."* (I John 4:18.)

It's Free!

When we were teens a phrase in a popular song repeatedly reminded us "the best things in life are free." Over the years I often found that true. Our family reunion was one such occasion.

Biannually, since 1986, G1adys and I have been blessed by being able to have all of our children and grandchildren together for a week. We've roamed the USA from the rolling hills of the Ozarks to the busyness of downtown Chicago to the tranquility of Andalusia, AL to the refreshing waters of the Gulf of Mexico.

In 1994 we spent a week in the Rocky Mountains. The camp offered a plethora of sports and recreational activities for the grandchildren. A kid's play paradise. No need to be bored. One day I asked some of them if they had ever played "kick the can," a game we (and maybe some of you) played as kids. Their puzzled looks indicated I was talking a foreign language. They were at home in the fast-paced world of computer games . . .

Little League baseball . . . and sensational TV programs. Kick the can? Sounds like 'Dullsville.'

They listened patiently as I explained the simple game. The only prop is an empty tin can. Someone is 'it' while the others hide. 'It' has to find them and when he/she spots someone, 'it' goes back to the can and calls "One, two, three, on . . ." When everyone is 'captured' someone else is 'it.' However, if someone "kicks the can" before 'it' gets there everyone is free and can go back into hiding. Then the routine starts over.

Being nice to Grandpa, they agreed to play . . . if . . . I would be 'it.' O.K. Instant success! Exciting! Addicting! The last three days we spent multi hours playing kick the can. Truth is, I never got out of being 'it.' What a great time we had playing a simple game. And all for free!

Sometime in our busyness or the pursuit of 'exciting' things to do we may overlook the common things . . . reading a story to a child . . . strolling on the beach . . . watching a gorgeous sunset . . . chatting over a cup of coffee with friends . . . walking in the rain. Not only are they free, but also they provide some of life's deepest pleasures.

Life is filled with the ordinary, but it becomes extraordinary when received as a gift from God. He *"richly provides us with everything for our enjoyment"* (I Timothy 6:17). We just need to take time to savor what he gives us so freely.

Honesty

A routine family prayer . . . a child's honesty . . . and some quiet reflection provided me with a timely reminder when our grandsons were younger.

Our son, Randy, was ready to lead us in prayer before our evening meal. Bonnie, our daughter- in-law, was at work. David and Nathan had walked to our house after school. Jonathan had spent a couple of hours at "Aunt Mary's", his occasional baby sitter. Gladys had picked Jonathan up, and after Randy arrived at our house we invited them to stay for a meal.

Randy's prayer began something like this:

"Dear Lord, thank you for this beautiful day . . . thank you for this good food . . . thank you that David and Nate had a good day in school . . . thank you that Jonathan did well at "Aunt Mary's" house . . .

"Wait a second, dad!" It was Jonathan interrupting emphatically. "I cried a few minutes at "Aunt Mary's" house.

Randy paused . . . made the correction, and then finished his prayer.

Here's a model for prayer I thought later. Jonathan had to set the record straight. It had gone well at "Aunt Mary's" house, but not totally well. There were a few tears. Jonathan knew it and <u>God</u> knew it! So, why pretend? Why not be honest before God? He also was very specific. No generalities. He cried. That was it. And he prayed without shame or fear. There was no doubt in his little mind that we, and especially God, would still love him.

How good it is to know that we can be honest in our prayers. We don't have to convince God that we have it altogether. Things are not always well within. We know it, and God knows it! That's o.k. We can also be specific. Generalities are easy; specifics bring healing. And we can pray confidently. God is our Father for Christ's sake. He'll never turn us away.

In the spirit of the Psalm writers we can bring everything to God . . . not only our praise and petitions . . . but also our flaws . . . and sins . . . and hurts. When we are honest . . . specific . . . and trusting . . . then we are truly praying, and our gracious God hears and responds. Like David we can say, *"I sought the Lord, and he answered me"* (Psalm 34:4).

Compassion

We ran the gamut of emotions as our five children went through the ritual known as "getting your driver's license." It was an interesting adventure.

Ron ushered us into this new world the first day he got his license. The 'little dent' from the parking ramp turned out to be a crease two inches deep and six feet long. Later he added to the drama by reorganizing the underside of a car on a tree stump. He capped it off by winning the MDV (Most Damaged Vehicle) honor when he totaled our station wagon.

Tom won the GBT (Gentle But Thorough) award. His five mishaps occurred while driving less than 5 miles an hour. On three occasions he backed into cars while pulling out of the driveway. He mangled the door of another person's car while parking, and for his final number graciously rearranged the side of our garage with the car door.

Jan's trophy was the LDV (Least Damaged Vehicle). Her only misdemeanor was a tiny scratch on our new

Impala. Ken was great! I gave him the TAL (Thanks A Lot) prize. He bought and smashed his own cars. Randy was runner-up to Ron's debacle with one major crash. I gladly gave him the TGIF (Thank Goodness It's Finished) medal.

How did I handle it all? Justly, I think, and with grace. They helped pay for the damages, but I kept blame and scolding to a minimum. This was confirmed later when Tom asked me why I showed such equanimity when confronted with the results of their blunders.

The answer was easy. I was only passing on what I had received. When my brother and I limped home with dented fenders, hanging bumpers, and smashed doors dad always handled it justly, and with grace. His attitude told us that he understood that these things happen, and that relationships are more important than cars. It was a powerful message – one that our children are passing on to their offspring.

My father's grace and understanding also helped me to understand God's grace and compassion in a deeper way. It was a real-life manifestation of the profound truth of Psalm 103: 13, *"As a father has compassion on his children, so the Lord has compassion on those who fear him."* His response gave me further insight into how God deals with us. How wonderful to serve a God who is patient with our foibles and sins and still loves us and uses us to accomplish his purpose in the world. He truly is able *"to sympathize with our weaknesses."* (Hebrews 4:15).

And he calls us to do the same with each other.

Today

For over 20 years my grandson, Nate, and I have blown out the candles on the cake as we celebrate our same-day birthday in January. "Best birthday present I ever had," I always tell him. It's a fun time for both of us. It's also a time for me to reflect on some interesting phases I've gone through in my lifetime.

Once upon a time I wanted to be older. At the magical age of 14 I became a licensed driver. (Yup, we were young drivers in the Stone Age). But I still envied 16 year olds, and at 16 I envied 18 year olds. Age 21 brought the privilege of voting. Getting older was cool.

But that changed. Looking young was in vogue for me. When our oldest son, Ron, was 2 or 3, a few people asked me if we were brothers. Wow! Thanks! When I served my first church people often told me I looked too young to be a pastor. Thanks again! Keep it coming.

Not for long. I soon entered a chronological no-man's land. Age wasn't much of a factor in my life. But the 15-

year hiatus ended when clerks and waitresses started to call me "sir." Middle age was beginning to show. At 55 I began to ask about senior discounts, but soon, to my chagrin, Mac Donald's waitresses gave me my "senior coffee" discount without my asking. That started a domino effect.

More change. Gradually people began to ask kindly and gently, and with some hesitancy, I must admit, whether I was retired. Ouch! Reality started to sink in. I'm really looking older. Then came the latest and last query: "How do you like retirement?" As an aside, I didn't fully retire until age 81.

I have concluded that it's a waste of energy **wishing** one were younger or older. No age is the perfect age. Each phase of life has some advantages and each has some disadvantages. It is much more important to focus on service to God and others at the present moment and in the present place. Enjoying the here and now is better than wishing for the then or when.

Our behavior . . . our decisions . . . our attitudes . . . today shape us as we grow older. The direction in which we are going is more important than the number of candles on our cake. As we focus on God . . . doing his will and enjoying his world . . . he promises to help us become wiser . . . more Christ-like . . . more useful . . . and more fulfilled. As we give ourselves to the present, getting older will take care of itself. I believe that is behind our Lord's reminder *"give us this day our daily bread"* (Matthew 6:11).

Reality

Gladys and I were motoring leisurely through the Rockies west out of Denver after spending an enjoyable 4 days with Tom and Luci, our son and daughter-in-law, and their family. Now we were on our way to California. The beauties around us - glistening green pines . . . majestic white-capped mountains . . . swirling emerald streams - all joined in an anthem of praise to our Creator. After two hours we stopped at a rest area and then strolled back to our rental car relaxed in body and calm in spirit.

We had driven only 100 feet when my calmness dissolved. My eye caught the gas gauge. Empty! Bone dry, it said. I nursed the car along as carefully as I could trying to conserve gas . . . 5 miles . . . then 10 . . . then 15 . . . then, at last . . . a station! I said a prayer of thanks as our thirsty tank began to lap up the gas. At 8 gallons it had enough. Whoa! This is a 20-gallon tank. Then I realized . . . the gauge was faulty. What I saw with my eye did not correspond to reality.

That can be true of life also at times. If we judge our lives by what we feel we can easily become discouraged. If we interpret the direction of the world by the sad events we see on television we could conclude that God is not in control. When we experience pain or we struggle in prayer we might think that God has left us. What _is_ the truth? What _is_ real?

The birth of Christ points us to reality. Our gauges, i.e., our feelings or our observations, can sometime be faulty. But Christ's coming tells us that God loves us and that he is always present with us. The incarnation is our assurance that God has not abandoned us and that he is in the process of making all things new. Jesus is *"the way and the truth and the life"* (John 14:6).

May that be your source of strength whenever you celebrate the birth of Jesus. And may you experience his joy as you share the good news with others.

Prepared

One of the joys Gladys and I have had as grandparents is watching our grandchildren compete in sports. We have run the gamut - basketball ... football ... softball ... baseball ... golf ... wrestling ... track ... swimming ... and soccer.

Playing sports requires some natural ability, of course, but it also requires the right equipment

I was reminded of that in a forceful and interesting way a number of years ago. In 1988 our son Tom moved to Denver, Colorado where he became pastor of Third Christian Reformed Church. We were there to help them unpack and be present for Tom's installation. On Monday morning our grandson Andy, age 4, asked if I wanted to play baseball with him. When I assented he went to get his shoes, put them on, and we played catch and I pitched the ball to him. On Tuesday morning he again wondered if I wanted to play ball with him. This time it was basketball. Once again he went away, came back carrying a pair of shoes, and after he put them on we went outside to shoot some hoops.

74

On Wednesday morning he greeted me early with shoes in hand. He told me these were his football shoes and asked if I wanted to play football this morning. I couldn't say no. So, we kicked and threw the football around. I woke up Thursday morning wondering what the sport would be. This time it was soccer. Now he had soccer shoes. Then I saw the pattern. Any old shoe wouldn't do. He had four pairs of shoes neatly lined up in his bedroom and he chose the right ones to fit the sport. He needed to be properly prepared and equipped.

There are occasions in life when we need to be properly prepared and equipped. We may be facing a difficult task . . . an unpleasant confrontation . . . or a complex decision. We may be unfairly criticized or receive bad news. There is an addiction that is hard to overcome. We may be going through a hard period where things just seem to pile up.

During those times we may feel we can't cope. We don't have the strength to endure. We may feel inadequate for the job. The enormity of the situation overwhelms us.

At times like this God promises to equip us and supply our needs. He may send a special friend to refresh us (I Corinthians 16:16). He provides words to speak when we need them (Luke 21:15). He supplies strength when we feel weak (Psalm 29:11). He bestows his grace just at the right time (II Corinthians 12:9). How great that we can join the Psalmist and say, *"Praise the Lord, O my soul, and forget not all his benefits"* (Psalm 103:2). His promise is always certain, *"I will be with you"* (Isaiah 43:2).

Staying Sharp

I had an "ou-ee." A cut thumb. Not too serious, but annoying. You have had cuts like that too so you know what I mean. There's some bleeding so you need a band-aid. It stings when you get water or juice in it. The band-aid comes off and needs replacing. It starts to heal, and then just as the scab forms you bump it and the bleeding starts again. So another band-aid and the whole process repeats itself, maybe a few more times. Gradually the slit closes up. The scab forms and finally drops off. Ah! My cut came while trying to slice a piece of summer sausage off a big roll so I could enjoy a sandwich. Evidently it didn't like the idea and it kicked the knife, which in turn did a job on my thumb.

That cut reminded me of cuts I used to get frequently during the 12 years I worked in a meat market. They went with the territory.

I remember one cut in particular because it came at such an inopportune time. It was about 5:30 in the afternoon. I was slicing some meat when the knife slipped. Bang. I cut about 1/16 of an inch off my middle finger on my right hand. Bah! I managed to get a bandage on it and stop the bleeding. But even worse than the cut, I was scheduled to play ball at 6:30. Oh, no! I was 17 at the time. To miss a game would have been a disaster. This was my life! What to do? In a stroke of genius I found a couple of pieces of wire and bent them to form a protective shield on the end of my finger. A few wraps of tape secured them in place, and I was able to play. Even got a couple of hits. The healing took two or three weeks and the scar disappeared over a period of time.

The eerie thing about all those cuts is that 95% of them occurred while I was using a <u>dull knife</u>. My mentor had warned me about this, but sometime I was too busy to take the time to sharpen the blade. Sure enough. Meat seems to recognize a dull edge. It fights and kicks and screams and then suddenly thrusts the blade into your finger or thumb.

There's a lesson here for us in our Christian walk. We have so many things to do and so many outside attractions. But in our busyness we may fail to take enough time with God. Then we lose our sharpness spiritually. The edge goes. We try to do it on our own. We end up with cuts and gouges.

The cure for spiritual dullness is to *"turn to the Lord"* (II Corinthians 3:14-18). Time spent in his presence through his Word and through prayer keeps us "sharp" for the task to which he has called us and helps us to grow stronger in our relationship to him.

In His Time

A church sign, a short side-street trip, and a yellow pages listing added up as one of God's surprises for Gladys and me in Florida a few years ago.

After a winter of 100 inches of snow, 32 consecutive days below freezing temperatures, and 5% sunshine we decided we needed a change The gorgeous Florida weather was just the cure for the malingering melancholy that menaces Michiganders in March.

We were also going through wintertime of the soul. Work related anxieties, unraveling relationships, and family health concerns had all converged on us within days of each other just before we left. We needed some respite to sort things out.

We arrived in Naples late Saturday afternoon and decided to attend a nearby Presbyterian church Sunday morning. As we rode by we noticed the hours of services were not posted and I told Gladys we could check that in the phone book later.

Following dinner we explored the town. When we returned to the hotel I checked the yellow pages under churches. The church we saw did not list the time of services. Then I recognized the name of another church I had seen on one of the many side streets we traversed in our tour of the city. We decided to go to the 10 a.m. service they listed.

Lloyd Ogilvie, the chaplain of the United States Senate was the guest preacher. God spoke to us in a most powerful way through his message based on Isaiah 26:3, *"You will keep him in perfect peace whose mind is steadfast, because he trusts in you."* Perfect timing! We felt God's peace warming our souls. "God's gift," Gladys whispered to me.

Later it all came together for me. The church of our choice had no times listed. Another one did. I could have turned unto many side streets, but I chose this one. There were many buildings, but I noticed the church. Coincidence? I think not. I'm not sure how it all works, but I know we were there by divine appointment. It was God's timing – his *"kairos,"* to use the biblical word. He knew exactly what we needed.

It's a comfort to know that in and through what seem like routine events in our lives God is at work. Even when it appears that things are working against us he is using small and innocuous incidents and weaving them into the pattern of his design. Truly, *"our times are in his hands"* (Psalm 31:15.) I am reminded of the words of Ecclesiastes 3:11 *"makes all things beautiful in its time."* What a great God we serve!

Gratitude

I find my motives for doing ministry can often be a mixed bag. Perhaps you do too as you seek to serve the Lord. We serve God, but we like people's applause. We display humility, but it's often tinged with pride. We work selflessly, but it's mingled with the need to validate ourselves. That's why it is appropriate at times to take inventory to determine our reasons for doing what we do. I was reminded of this in a conversation I had when my mother passed away.

Among the people who came to express condolences were long-time friends of my parents, John and Anne. And true friends they were. When my father was sick they drove my mother to the hospital and stayed to visit him. After my father passed away they stayed in contact with my mother. Anne would wash and set her hair and they took care of other chores for her. When I saw them at the funeral home I expressed my thanks for all they had done for my parents.

John modestly told me that it hadn't been that much. He explained how they moved from Iowa to Grand Rapids, MI. to escape the 'Dust Bowl,' that awful period in the late 30s and early 40s when a combination of severe drought and high winds scattered thousands of acres of rich topsoil from many Midwest states to states far east of the Mississippi River.

They arrived in Grand Rapids penniless and went to my father's grocery store to ask if they could get some groceries on credit. Your dad willingly gave us what we needed, John related, even though he was as poor as we were. We wouldn't have eaten without his help. We've always been grateful and that's why it's always been easy to help them.

Gratitude is a primary rationale for serving our Lord. We show we are thankful when our deeds are a response to what God has done for us through his son, Jesus. *"Thanks be to God for his indescribable gift"* (II Corinthians 9:15). We display it as we are faithful in the daily routine of our service ... go the extra mile ... show compassion ... and maintain our integrity at all times.

Living out of thankfulness can help us to resist acting out of the wrong motives. It helps us uproot the temptation to ingratiate people . . . to prove ourselves . . . or to get our own way in life. A life of gratitude means we stay focused on God and his work in our lives. Christian living, as a response to his grace and love, is fruitful . . . satisfying . . . and lasting.

In God's Hand

In 1998 we went on a safari in Kenya with our friends, Jim and Judy DeVries. For ten days we traversed this vast country tracking a wide variety of animals and birds. Each day brought new excitement and wonder as we watched lumbering elephants, graceful cheetahs, majestic lions, mischievous warthogs and many other wild animals in their natural habitat. We never tired of seeing the exotic birds - mufti-colored superb starlings, lilac-breasted crowned rollers, sand grouses, and over 70 others that we identified. This once-in-a-lifetime experience is permanently etched in our memories!

Adding to our delight were the times our guide, Mohamed, shared tidbits of information with us about the economy of the animal system. One instance occurred when we spotted a herd of giraffes feasting on the leaves of the trees. As these graceful ruminants stretched their long slender necks to reach the top branches as high as 15 to 16 feet off the ground, our guide pointed out that the trees are never stripped bare as the giraffes forage for food. Later he explained why.

We drove up close to a whispering thorn (or gall acacia) tree, a favorite of giraffes. Mohamed pointed out little nodules on the branches inhabited by colonies of ants. As the giraffes shake the branches while devouring the leaves, the alarmed ants leave their domicile and bite the lips and nose of their tormentors. In self-protection the giraffes move on to another part of the tree where the process is repeated. Meanwhile, many of the leaves are spared.

The entire interaction, it struck me, was a combination of frustration and provision. The trees were being stripped of their leaves . . . the ants were threatened . . . the giraffes were bitten . . . <u>frustration!</u> But there was another side . . . <u>provision!</u> The tree was spared total damage, yet still furnished food for the giraffe and shelter for the ants . . . the ants protected the tree and also found refuge in its branches . . . the giraffes found the victuals they needed. Behind it all is a wise God at work.

Isn't that same mixture found in life? We all know <u>frustration</u> . . . hassles with people . . . lack of results . . . loss of dreams . . . plans that go awry . . . goals not reached. It's easy to focus on them. But there's a bigger picture. God is at work. There is <u>provision!</u> He understands our frustrations, and he often works through them for our good. We may be led down new paths where we experience forced growth . . . a deeper faith . . . renewed relationships . . . a larger vision of God. Remember, just as the animals and nature are in his hands, so are we. *"Ask the animals, and they will teach you . . . in his hand is the life of every creature and the breath of all mankind"* (Job 12:7, 10).

Green Pastures

Events on a hot July day . . . a pleasant month of October . . . and a cold December morning all in the year 2003 came together to usher in a surprising and blessed change in my life.

I preached in a Grand Rapid church on one of those hot, humid days where every conversation begins "Sure is hot today." The air-conditioned church helped us to forget the weather and focus on God. After the service Gladys and I chatted for some time with a couple from our former church in Ann Arbor, Michigan who were visiting their son's family. They had come to this church because their son's church was without air and they wanted to be comfortable in worship. They also invited me to preach in our former church in October. The month long preaching in Ann Arbor was an enriching and blessed experience.

One cold December evening I preached in another Grand Rapids Church. On Monday morning as Gladys and I were eating breakfast I remarked to her that this was the first time in over 44 years in ministry that I did not have some speaking engagement ahead in my schedule. Since entering the ministry there has always been preaching, retreats, and other speaking opportunities on the horizon. Now the cupboard was bare. I felt a tinge of sadness, but I agreed it was reality. Gladys was more optimistic. "I don't think God is through with you yet," she said. Her words were prophetic.

On Thursday morning of that week an elder from the Ann Arbor Church called to offer me the position of interim Pastor of Preaching for 6 months beginning January 1, 2004. After prayer and some deliberation I accepted the offer. So, in addition to our Paraklesis work, each weekend we commuted to Ann Arbor. The 6 months turned into 18 months. That period was followed by 13 months in another church in Grand Rapids . . . 6 months in another church in Grand Ledge, Michigan . . . and 4 years of ministry in still another church in Grand Rapids.

Gladys was right. God was not through with us yet. .

When I think back on all that happened, two thoughts from the Psalm 23 come to my mind.

One, <u>God leads</u>. "*. . . he guides me in paths of righteousness*" (verse 3b). I did not choose the next 8 years of my life. God was going ahead of me. I trust you can say that also as you look back on events of your life and see the hand of God leading you.

Two, <u>God refreshes</u>. "he *makes me to lie down in green pastures*" (verse 2). Those eight years have been a time of refreshment and growth for both of us. Isn't it great to know that in the busyness of life and the demanding routine we face that our Shepherd is going ahead of us and finding those places and times where we can be refreshed and encouraged. He is constantly looking out for us and then in his timing brings us to 'green pastures. Be assured that God is not through with you yet and will also provide and renew you as he leads you along

Faithfulness

I have always had ambivalent feelings about cats and dogs. I am certain there are a lot of 'special pets' out there. The truth is, there are only two cats and four dogs that I am really fond of. For the rest, I guess I just tolerate them. Yet, I remember an incident with a lost cat vividly.

While working in the yard when we lived in Cleveland I heard a baby-like cry. Upon investigation I discovered a Siamese cat had fallen into one of our window wells and was unable to get out. What to do? Take it out and release it? Or, care for it and find the owner? My pastoral instincts overruled my natural inclination. I brought it in the house and soothed it the best I could.

Recognizing it was a beautiful and expensive cat I decided to place an ad in the lost and found section of the Cleveland paper. For the next five days our phone rang incessantly. I lost track of the number of calls, but it seemed like at least 847,303 people in Cleveland had lost a Siamese cat – one more than the population of the entire city. When I described the cat most people knew it was not theirs. The people who came to look didn't recognize it as their cat either.

About a week after the arrival of our new boarder a lady a few streets away called to ask if she could see the cat. Her children had heard about the cat in school. She knocked at our back door and I welcomed her into the kitchen. I'll never forget what happened next. The cat was across the kitchen about twenty feet away. The lady saw the cat and tapped lightly on her chest. Instantly the cat scrambled across the room and in one gigantic leap nestled securely on the lady's chest. There was no doubt whose cat this was. We were both happy . . . she because she had her cat; I because the cat was gone.

What struck me was that there was a relationship between the lady and her cat that was never broken while they were apart. It was evident they had a strong bond which couldn't be severed by their physical separation. And when they came together they connected immediately.

So it is with our relationship with God. At times we feel distant from God. In difficult times we may feel he has abandoned us. Sometime in our busyness we fail to be aware of his presence. We all experience times of spiritual drought. A desert experience makes us wonder where God is. The truth is, he is always there. *"Never will I leave you. Never will I forsake you"* (Hebrews 13:5). Ever so faithfully he seeks us . . . calls us back . . . and finds us. And when he does, we know it!

Truth

On various occasions over the years I get together with my siblings. Inevitably we take time to look back with more mature eyes on some of our past joys, struggles, and squabbles. And, of course, we talk about our parents. They were dear people – hard-working . . . God-fearing "salt of the earth" folks, whose love for us was reciprocal.

I remember one time relating an incident when a salesman came to our store and offered my father some beautiful picture frames, all at the unbelievably low price of $ 2.00. He suggested that we could put a $ 3.99 price tag on them and slash that through. Then they could be "marked down" to $ 2.99. As a 13 year old I thought it was an outstanding idea. We would have a 33% markup and people would think they were getting a 25% discount.

To my utter amazement my father vetoed the idea. He said he'd put $ 2.99 on them right away. I wondered how my dad could be so naïve and unsophisticated.

How could he so quickly dismiss this brilliant strategy? I didn't understand.

Some years later I did. My father made his decision because he was a man of truth. He could not in good conscience do something that even <u>hinted</u> at being misleading. There had not been an original $ 3.99 price tag. How could he pretend there was?

Truthfulness speaks of integrity, wholeness, and honesty. It is congruence between our private self and our public self. It is be able to say as the Apostle Paul did, "My conscience is clear" (I Corinthians 4:4). To live truthfully means to live life from the inside out.

Truth is a paramount virtue in all of life. I believe truth is the *sine- qua- non* of life. Being truthful helps us make decisions for the right reasons. It enables us to hold up under the withering fire of criticism. Truthfulness makes us "believable." People know we care.

Living truthfully is not always easy in our sinful world. The temptation to hide our true selves, to cut corners, and to shade the truth is always nearby. Our need to be liked and our fear of failure can often make us less than truthful with ourselves and others.

That's why it's important that we echo the prayer of the Psalmist, *"Teach me your way, O Lord, and <u>I will walk in your truth</u>; <u>give me an undivided heart</u>, that I may fear your name.* (Psalm 86:11). We cannot manufacture truthfulness on our own. It is a gift God gives as we seek it and live close to him. And we know, because he is the God of truth, that he will hear us and give us what we need.

Relief

As our children were growing up I often assumed a quasi-physician's role by tending to sundry hurts and scrapes, bandaging bloody fingers or legs, and peering into mouths and ears.

There was one time, however, when I had to go beyond the routine 'doctor' duties. Late one summer evening we were shutting some of our windows because rain had been forecast. As I lowered the dining room window I heard an agonizing 'ouch!' from the kitchen. One of our ancient windows decided to take the fast lane down and landed smack on Gladys' finger.

By the time I got there her fingernail was already turning purple. The pain became more intense as the blood tried to squeeze into a place it wasn't meant to be. This needed more than just a little soaking in ice. I quickly called our family doctor who told me I could assuage her pain by taking a razor blade, sterilizing it, and gradually cutting through the nail.

I admit, I kind of relished my new role. Gladys looked away as I made my first imprint on her nail. I worked into a rhythm. Methodically . . . carefully . . . I moved the blade back and forth. Suddenly . . . a red gusher! The blood spurted freely over our hands and the kitchen table. Then I heard a most satisfying sound: Gladys' big 'aaaaahhhhh' of relief. The pressure was gone! The cause of her agony had been exorcised. In a few days, with the help of pain pills, she was on the mend.

Emotional pressures can also be a source of pain. An unconfessed sin rambling in our hearts causes a constant inner ache. A bad habit we refuse to confront seeps some of the joy out of life. A broken relationship leaves a wound that never quite heals. A hurt inflicted by some careless word or deed gnaws away at our self-worth. When we fail to address these issues properly the pressure mounts. The result may be unhealthy behavior, physical illness, or depression.

Thank God there is a way out. The strain can be released. We can bring it to him for he is *"the God who heals us"* (Exodus 15:26). God also provides people who love . . . who care . . . and listen . . . and understand.

What a relief when we let them come along side of us and help us *"carry the burden"* (Galatians 6:2).

If you are dealing with some internal pain I encourage you to bring it in the open and let God begin the healing process. He can be trusted to be gentle and kind as you experience his care.

Abundance

Help can sometime come from unexpected sources. I learned that in a not-to-be-forgotten way in my first year of ministry.

A doctor who had just joined our church asked me to offer the opening prayer at a prestigious convention of doctors in New Jersey. I could either take a ferry or the Walt Whitman Bridge over the Schuylkill River from Philadelphia where we lived. The ferry was ½ hour shorter but cost $2.00; taking the bridge cost $.50. Living on the edge of poverty, but also wanting to save some time, I decided to take the ferry on the way over and the bridge on the way back.

I checked my wallet as I was leaving. Whoops. I had only $ 2.00 and some change. Not enough. Too late to take the bridge over. Gladys had a few coins, but I was still short. Don't panic I told myself. Like the woman in the parable we searched the house carefully. We found a few coins under the cushions of our easy chairs. The kids' piggy banks yielded a couple more. Stay cool, I reminded myself. Ha! I was 4 cents short. What to do? Asking my host for a nickel would be embarrassing. Our checkbook said zilch. Looks like I'd have to walk in late with a red face.

Ah . . . then I remembered. A few days earlier our son, Tom, had dropped pennies down the slot of the window defroster in the car. Maybe, just maybe, they'd be accessible. A few quick turns of the screwdriver and I had loosened the frame around the windshield. A gold mine! Not one, not two, not four, but six pennies. Superabundance! Two more than I needed! Thank you, Lord. I made the ferry in the nick of time, offered a gracious prayer, enjoyed a delicious meal, and took the longer route home.

I've had other times when I have been perplexed, of course. Many times on a more serious level. I'm certain you know what I mean. Sometime there seems to be no way out of a situation. Illness can be a time like that, or . . . we feel estranged from a friend or a loved one . . . we go through a time of discouragement . . . finances are at a breaking point.

Then in some unexpected way God provides. Through unexpected ways he ministers to us. Someone speaks just the words we need to hear. An unexpected gift arrives. An unexpected note brightens the day. Sometime he gives us even more than we need, be it two pennies. God can *"turn darkness into light"* (Psalm 18:28). That's his message to us – a message we are also privileged to share with others.

Likeness

I went grocery shopping with my daughter, Jan, some time ago. As a former grocery store owner I like to see how much things have changed and how much they've remained the same since my long-gone days behind the counter. We meandered up and down the aisles filling the shopping cart with items on her list and also doing a little impulse buying. Somehow sweets and other goodies are more tempting when you're with someone else.

When we reached the checkout Jan began putting her purchases on the counter. Suddenly she turned around with a sly grin on her face and a twinkle in her eye. "Dad," she said trying to sound disgusted, "I realize I'm becoming more and more like you." When I asked why, her grin widened. "I'm getting too organized. I'm placing all the goods on the counter so the price codes are visible for the clerk and she can scan them more easily." She paused a few moments to let it sink in. Then came the punch line. "It really scares me," she said with a smile.

Jan and I have a lot of traits in common . . . sometime to our delight . . . sometime to our chagrin. As I see her interaction with people . . . her response to situations . . . her motivational attractions . . . and her perception on problems, I often see myself.

I'm sure the same is true in your family. Children mirror parents in many ways whether or not they like it. Foibles and strengths become a part of the next generation. Through nature and nurture a constant shaping process is taking place.

The Scriptures tell us that a greater shaping is taking place in all of us. We are continually being *"conformed to the likeness Of Christ"* (Romans 8:29). Through the experiences of life and the power of the Holy Spirit we are in the process of becoming what God wants us to be. Each day with its pain . . . its pleasure . . . its joy . . . its sorrow . . . its drudgery . . . and its delights is being used by God to mold and fashion us after the semblance of Jesus.

While we carry out our busy agendas God is working out a deeper agenda. Even those days when we think we've accomplished nothing God has nudged us in his direction. And . . . when the final chapter is written we will fully realize what God did <u>to</u> us is more important than what he did <u>through</u> us. Then, we *"shall be like him"* forever (I John 3:2). That's not scary. That's grace!!

Appearances

All of us have our embarrassing moments. One of mine came a few years prior to leading an evening worship service. After arriving at the church I met with 5 or 6 elders preceding the service to go over the order of worship and also for prayer.

We stood together in a side room and engaged in some small talk. I went over the service with one of the elders and then it was time to pray. As I bowed my head I made a startling discovery. My shoes didn't match! Horrors! While reaching in my closet to get dressed I had picked up one shoe from one pair and a second shoe from another. Although they have about the same shape one is brown and the other cordovan. Can you imagine a preacher whose shoes don't match?

Instant panic! In a split second I conjured up a hundred ideas to avoid looking foolish. I could call attention to it and make a joke of it before someone else did. When seated on the platform I could sit on one foot. While preaching I could stand on one leg and hide the offending shoe behind it. I could distract people by pulling my handkerchief part way out of my pocket. I could pretend to have an urgent appointment after the service and have to leave immediately. The ideas flowed like water from a burst dam. Pressure begets creativity.

Before the elder finished praying I recovered my sanity and added a silent prayer that God would help me to do what needed to be done . . . lead his people in worship. If I focused on appearances I would lose the reason I had come for.

Thank God I was able to concentrate fully on the service. I even stayed in the narthex after the service for coffee and visiting. If anyone noticed, they were gracious enough to say nothing.

It's easy to buy into our culture's obsession with appearances. After all, who doesn't want to look good? There's the temptation to cover our mistakes . . . to pretend we have all the answers . . . to come off as always competent. But in our preoccupation with striving to look good we fool only ourselves. Trying to impress means diverting too much energy to what is secondary. We may be tuning out God's call because we don't want people to have a poor impression of us.

God does not condone sloppiness. But looking good is not primary with him. The Scriptures remind us *"Man looks at outward appearance. God looks at the heart"* (I Samuel 16:7). We all have our unmatched shoes. But God can and does use us when we are in step with him.

God's Plans

I did something almost unthinkable a few years ago. Even as I write this I can't believe I did it. My "horrible" deed? I threw away a map!! It was a dilapidated California map that I got free from a Standard gas station about 30 years before. It was hopelessly outdated and tattered. I have newer ones. But it was a map. Parting with it just didn't seem right. Only after some deep soul-searching and hesitation could I put it in the recycling bin.

I've always been fascinated by maps. Whether I'm planning a trip or just want to relax, perusing a map serves the purpose. There are three reasons maps give me enjoyment.

One, maps give directions. Maps show me the best route to take to reach my destination. Once I study a map I have the gift of assimilating it my mind. I find it makes for more relaxing and enjoyable driving. Maps help me avoid aimless wandering.

Two, maps also help me recall happy occasions. As I read maps I relive our fall trips through the colorful mountains of New England. I hear anew the surging of an angry ocean pounding the rocky shore in Nova Scotia. I see the splendor of the Taj Mahal in India. I feel the warm sun on the beach in Hawaii. I revisit Stone Henge in England.

Three, maps take me to new places. In Switzerland I noticed on the map a scenic side road that would still take us to our destination. We ended up staying the night in a picture post-card village with a view of the mountains we would never forget

It strikes me that what maps do for us on one level God does on a much higher plane.

One, God gives us precise directions for our lives in a variety of ways. He spells out his expectations in his Word. He tells us what is right and wrong. He clearly marks out paths that lead to life and those that lead to self-harm. He defines reality for us.

Two, God has also given us the gift of memory. We recall his work in our lives. He reminds us when he walked with us through troubled times. He jogs our memory as we relive mountain-top experiences we have had with him. We remember his faithfulness.

Three, God also steers us to new paths. Ministry doors open up that we haven't even dreamed about. We meet new people who fill our lives with peace and blessing. Opportunities to grow come in unexpected ways. He often "surprises us with joy," to quote C.S. Lewis.

How wonderful it is to know that we do not just wander aimlessly through life. We are in the hands of the one who says carries out *"the plans he has for us"* (Jeremiah 29:11). Truly, *"in him in whom we live and move and have our being"* (Acts 17:28).

God's Leading

The monkeys and chimps provided first-rate entertainment in our visit to the John Ball Zoo one Labor Day with our grandson Jonathan, who was 5 at the time We watched with delight and laughed out loud as they nimbly skipped from limb to limb, walked thin ropes with no fear, nibbled at their bits of lettuce, and nudged each other for top position on the pole. It was a fascinating sight for all ages.

Gladys and I also reminisced as we watched their amazing acrobatic antics. It was at this exact spot, monkey island, where we met almost 64 years ago on Labor Day.

My friend, Pete, and I did the usual young guy thing on Labor Day in '48. We sat around a while, had some snacks, rode on his moped and took in a movie. But by seven o'clock we decided we needed some excitement. Perhaps we could meet some young ladies. But where would we find them? Aha! At John Ball Park where the Christian Labor Union was holding a rally. We nonchalantly meandered through the crowd looking for some possibilities. Our prospects looked bleak until we spotted two girls walking toward the zoo. This could be our moment. We took off *post haste*.

Our pace slowed as we closed the gap. Had to be cool, you know. Neither too eager nor too timid. Appearance was crucial. As we edged closer we agreed I should initiate the conversation. Since I was the taller of the two I would try to get the attention of the taller young lady. Drawing on all the charm and wisdom of my 17 years I said something certain to find favor in the ears of any attractive female. Sure enough, she turned and we started talking. We've been talking for the past 63 plus years. Gladys was the taller one.

It's interesting that I made my choice just on the information I had. I only knew she was the taller of the two girls. Yet God used this one factor to bring us together.

When we have to make decisions we usually like to have all the facts before us. If we don't, we often like God to zap us with some quick answer. But sometime neither happens. We have only a little bit of information.

I have learned through our Labor Day encounter and other incidents that God guides us when <u>we are on the way</u>. Even though we may not see everything clearly, when we go in faith on the information we have, God will be there to direct our paths. He may open or close doors. He may give new insights. He may provide new skills. However he leads we know he is there for us. We have his assurance, *"I will guide you in the ways of wisdom and lead you along straight paths"* (Proverbs 4:11).

Love

I can remember the scene so well. I was standing on emotional tiptoes by the nursery window in the Hospital waiting to catch a glimpse of Ron, our first born, who had arrived just a few moments before. Gladys had endured the rigors of pregnancy as well as can be expected. The labor room had been seven hours of pains . . . reassuring doctors doing their exams . . . cheerful nurses giving shots and dispensing meds . . . some talking and also times of silence. But now, the gift for which we had waited nine months was here!

The nursery contained an assortment of babies of sundry sizes, shapes and hues. But I was interested in only one. Through the pane of glass I caught the eye of a nurse in the back of the room drying off a baby she had just washed. Her smile told me it was he! Bingo! After weighing him, she cradled Ron in her arms and then brought him, sans a stitch of clothing, to the window for my first close up look. There he was, all 5 1/2 pounds of him!

Someone else would probably have seen nothing but a long, skinny, bellowing batch of protoplasm . . . bony ribs . . . reed-thin arms . . . toothpick-size fingers . . . and gangly legs. Instead of hair there was just a hint of peach fuzz. His nose was bent to one side. His left ear was pinned almost flat to the side of his head. People would probably mutter politely, "Nice baby."

That's not what I saw! I saw the most beautiful baby I had ever seen!! I saw a miracle God had allowed us to bring into the world. I saw our son! I saw a boy who would eventually smile at me . . . a lad with whom I would play ball . . . a son who would call me "dad"! I saw him not with my physical eyes, but with the eyes of my heart!

That's also how God sees us - with the eyes of His heart. It's easy for us to focus on our failures and limitations. We tend to define ourselves by what we are not. We see scars and blemishes. But God sees us as we really are. We are his children! His sons and daughters! Because we are in Christ he says to us also, *"You are my child whom I love; with you I am well pleased"* (Matthew 3:17).

That's our true status. With that assurance we can live effectively and joyfully in our Father's world.

Someday

One of the highlights of our camping days was the evening campfire. After a day of swimming, fishing, hiking, lying around, and eating, we gathered for our daily ritual around the fire pit. We took some wood from home, but much of it we collected in walks through the woods and around the grounds. Gladys was a master at spotting fuel for the conflagration. Thanks to her eagle eye, like the widow's oil, our supply never dwindled.

After one of the children built a teepee of kindling and other wood and lit it, we watched as the hesitant flames evolved to maturity. A one-match fire was a victory. Then our senses came alive. We were mesmerized by the reflection of the dancing flame in each other's eyes. Our olfactory nerves savored the aroma of burning wood. We listened with delight to the crackling blaze and an occasional popping log. Our talk time was interspersed with moments of silence. Crickets chirped and frogs croaked in the background.

When someone suggested we make s'mores the vote was always unanimous. Nothing could top a sandwich of graham crackers, roasted marshmallows and a piece of Hershey's chocolate. Our time gathered around the fire-ring was a great way to end the day.

There was a frequent annoyance, however. Often a wisp of smoke would head directly for one of us. Whoever was the target would move. But then the pesky vapor either found a new prey or relentlessly pursued the initial victim. We realized this would happen sporadically, and we learned to accept it as a part of camp life.

The warm (no pun intended) memories of those halcyon times remind me that many of life's greatest pleasures are often found in simple things. The ordinary is often the milieu where we experience some of our most precious moments. A baby's smile . . . a birthday celebration . . . an unexpected phone call . . . a sincere thank you . . . or an 'I love you' can often bring us greater joy than expensive toys or elaborate undertakings.

I'm also reminded that life has annoyances. Someone doesn't show up on time. It rains when we want to be outdoors. Someone gets sick at the wrong time. Delays force us to alter travel plans. We have misunderstandings. While God doesn't send us these annoyances, I believe they are his way of reminding us that this life can never fully satisfy us. Only he can do that.

Here's the good news. Someday all irritations will disappear. Someday everything will be the way it's supposed to be. According to his promise some day we will inherit *"a new heaven and a new earth"* (Revelation 21:1). In the meantime we can relish the gifts he gives us. And we need to pray for grace to accept petty vexations for what they are.

Guidance

Do you remember learning to whistle? What an accomplishment! First you pursed your lips and blew and blew. Nothing but air. Perhaps a little humming would help. No go. You persisted. Finally, a faint peep. A whistle in the larva stage. Gradually you mastered the intricacies of whistling. You could even carry a tune. Another step along the road to adulthood.

My whistling career didn't plateau there. I learned what I called the "wailer." That's the one where you cup your hands together and blow between your thumbs. Skillfully done you can sound like anything from a train whistle to a dog in heat. I graduated *magna cum laude*.

The peak of my whistling career, however, occurred when I mastered the "screecher." No mean accomplishment. You put two fingers from each hand in your mouth and by positioning your tongue in just the right way you can emit a shrill sound that will put a hole through steel.

The "screecher" became a valuable tool as our children grew up. Often at dinnertime they would be scattered through the neighborhood, but when I called them their names evaporated into thin air. So I'd be a one-man search party until I found them. Then I hit on an idea. The "screecher" would be a generic signal for all of them to come home. Success! A couple of good blasts and, if they were within two blocks of home, they would soon wander in. 95% success rate.

What strikes me is that they *"knew"* it was for them. They never heard their names called. They couldn't see me. Yet they responded. No mistake. They *"knew"* it was dad calling.

There are times when that happens in our relationship to God. You hear no audible voice. You see no angelic visitor . . . no neon sign . . . no opening of the sky, but deep in your heart you *"know"* that God has spoken to you. No one else may hear it, or recognize it, but you *"know"* it is the Lord. It may come as a call to seek a new vocation. It may be a nudging to contact a certain person. Sometime it is the conviction that a decision is right. It may be an overwhelming assurance that you are

God's child. Deep down you recognize your Father's voice. Indelibly etched in the soul is the certainty that God has moved toward you in a special way.

What a blessing to serve a God who promises *"I will instruct you and teach you in the way you should go"* (Psalm 32:8), and then keeps that promise.

Prayer

It was a fitting illustration used by our guest preacher to encourage us to bring <u>everything</u> to God in prayer. A couple prayed earnestly and regularly that their 12-year-old daughter would find a friend when they moved to a new neighborhood. Sure enough, within a few months a 12-year-old girl moved into a vacant house two doors away. The girls enjoyed their friendship all through high school. It's heartening to hear stories like that. God does answer prayer!

As Gladys and I listened to the story we both had the same thoughts, and we knowingly nudged each other. That was our story . . . except for one twist! Jan was 11 years old when we moved to Ann Arbor from Cleveland. Since there were no girls her age in the neighborhood we too prayed earnestly and regularly for a girl her age to move into the vacant house across the street.

We watched eagerly. Finally the "for sale" sign came down . . . the moving van arrived . . . the family pulled up . . . and then . . . an answer to prayer! They had a girl

Jan's age. God is so good! A few days later Gladys took Jan across the street and introduced her to her new neighbor.

Did you ever have it where you met someone and absolutely nothing happened? No vibes . . . no connection . . . no feeling of kindred spirits. Just a deep void . . . a wide chasm . . . a broad moat? Well, that's what happened here. The girls exchanged pleasantries and then never said a word or paid attention to each other for the entire 5 years we lived there.

For us that raised some questions about prayer . . . questions I'm sure you have asked too. Why one answer for us, and another for them? Were we less sincere? Did we have the wrong formula? Does God answer or refuse prayers based on a whim? Does he respond capriciously to the prayers of his people? Does prayer really matter? Is there an answer?

The lesson we learned, and are continuing to learn, is that God remains faithful no matter what the outcome is. He said to Paul, and to all of us, *"My grace is sufficient for you"* (II Corinthians 12:9). All he asks is that we trust him . . . that we reach out in faith and put ourselves in his hands. As we do that we continually experience his abiding presence. Our faith is not based on answers to prayer, but on the very character of God. And we know he can be trusted. What a privilege to know him . . . and to do his work in this world.

Life's Viruses

I battled a nasty virus some time ago. Well, it was a computer virus actually, but I may as well have had it personally.

It all started in June when I received a request via email to look at an attached proposal. It turned out to be an engineering proposal. Mistaken address probably. After a few similar missives that day I wrote the sender about his mix-up. As the avalanche of proposals continued I wondered if some residual effects of my A- average in trig and geometry courses in college had reached the engineering world. Maybe he did want my opinion.

My balloon was soon punctured as I began receiving mail from people who told me to stop sending them mail. This hooked into my neurotic need to be liked so I sent letters of apology, still not realizing what was happening. Finally the lights went on. It was a virus. I had become another victim of someone's need to be mean.

My computer guru cleaned up the virus and I downloaded a more powerful antivirus program. Safe at last! Then, one fateful day, a few months later I innocently opened an attachment from someone whose name was familiar. There was nothing in it so I went merrily on my way. Then the nasty letters to stop sending email came again. So, back to the shop for a clean-up. Free again! I breathed a sigh of relief. Two days later the bottom fell out. Letters and phone calls indicated a third virus. Bah!

Now I started talking to myself. I should seek some kind of revenge. I didn't deserve this. I'd get even, somehow. Fortunately, my brain kicked in. Sure it was a nuisance, but not a catastrophe. Things could be worse. Life goes on. So, again I had the computer cleaned up and a better antivirus program installed. To this date the infection has been cured.

I've been thinking about other types of "viruses" that can affect our lives. They creep into our systems and disrupt our lives and make us less productive. Some examples are overworking . . . criticism . . . disrupted relationships . . . family antagonism . . . unhealthy habits

. . . secret sins   . . . procrastination . . . and misplaced anger. All can keep us from being effective instruments of God's grace and mercy.

While these "viruses" are sometime unavoidable, many can be prevented. Some of our difficulties stem from an inner restlessness and emptiness. Our behavior can become a way of trying to assuage the pain and discomfort we feel. But it's the wrong antidote. The true remedy is the inner peace that only God can give. Jesus said, *"Come to me and I will give you <u>rest</u>"* (Matthew 11:28). When he stills the storm within us, he enables us to meet the outside storms in healthier ways. In your busyness be sure to spend time with him.

Rewards

Faster! Stronger! Higher! The Olympic flame, fueled by a volatile mixture of commercialism and athleticism, burns brightly throughout the world for 17 days in July and August every four years. It is, to say the least, a spectacular event. It also reminds me of my own participation in the Olympics.

My attempt at Olympic competition occurred when I entered into one of those magical ages of life. Remember when you couldn't wait to be 16? and then 18? and then 21? Real life started, many of us thought, beyond those barriers. Well, I can remember when I hit 50 - another significant milestone. Days Inn invited me to join their September Club. Ugh. The American Association of Retired People offered so many discounts I thought merchants would end up paying me. And, I was eligible for the Senior Olympics!

Being a person of modest athletic skills I decided to enter two events, the 50-yard dash and the basketball free throw. I paced off 50 yards in front of our house and past our neighbor's house. Like Forest Gump I ran and ran and ran. I imagined the headlines: "50 year old breaks world record." I shot baskets in the backyard *ad nauseum.* On the day of competition I was ready!

Ten yards down the straightaway I felt a sharp twinge in my leg. My 50-year-old brain told me to quit. I listened. But there was still the free throw competition. Despite the light balls and a slight breeze I managed to hit nothing but net on quite a few of my shots. I waited for the medals to be handed out late in the afternoon. Track. Swimming. Then, basketball. No gold. No silver. And the bronze medal winner is..... Sid Draayer. Yes! After hours of work I had my reward.

Rewards are also one of the blessings of the Christian life. Even though we don't work for that reason God gives them to us. All our work, our fears, our hassles, our prayers are not in vain. In his own way God uses them to change lives . . . to lift burdens . . . to redirect people . . . to bring healing. There is the satisfaction of knowing that somehow I have made a difference.
Unlike Olympic medals our rewards endure. My medal hangs on a nail in a 3' by 3' closet we call the bottle

room where it shares space with empty bottles, old newspapers, cleaning rags and sundry odds and ends. Our reward is one *"that will never fade away"* (*I* Peter 5: 4). May that promise be your encouragement and your incentive to be faithful at all times.

Dependence

Isn't it interesting that many things that are good and give us pleasure can also be a source of anxiety and frustration? Children are one example; airplanes are another.

I'm fascinated by airplanes. To me they are a rare combination of grace, power, speed, and utility. My Walter Mitty fantasy is to take off and land as the pilot of a 747. I'm still amazed that I can sit in a plane with a minimum of discomfort and then in a few hours cross six time zones, span an ocean, and be in a completely different culture and land. What a boon to travel airplanes are!

But there's also the other side. I learned it well on one occasion when I flew to our daughter Jan's house in Alabama. I took jets from Grand Rapids to Detroit to Memphis. In Memphis, I boarded a smaller plane - a prop job . . . 30 passenger capacity . . . coffee served out of a thermos . . . a dwarf among giants on the runway. I had the exit row with two seats. I snoozed a few minutes after we took off, and then became absorbed in my book. The two engines hummed quietly as we made our way south.

An hour into the flight my inner calm was shattered. My untrained ear picked up that the engine just outside my window was not running smoothly. I got back to my book and then took another glance outside. Whoa! The engine had stopped. Instant response!! Blood pressure up . . . heart rate up . . . endocrine glands shooting adrenalin all through my body . . . white knuckles gripping the armrest. A few moments later the pilot assured us we would easily make it to Mobile on only one engine. The fire trucks and emergency equipment we would see were only a precaution. Whoops! More adrenaline. I pretended to read for the last 15 minutes of the flight, but I could only concentrate on one thing - the other engine! We landed without incident. Praise God!

The predominant feeling I had through all this, I realized on reflection, was the sense of complete dependency - on the pilot . . . on the second engine . . .

and ultimately on God. There was nothing any of us on the plane could do. Things were out of our hands.

Isn't that a parable of life itself? Not only on airplanes, but, where ever we are and whatever we do we are completely dependent on God. *"In him we live and move and have our being"* (Acts 17:28). We need to be aware of that constantly. More importantly, the God on whom we are dependent for everything is always dependable. That's the good news! That's the gospel!

Co-workers

While going through the laborious task of packing and unpacking boxes and hauling furniture when we moved our office, I also took the time to clean out some files.

When I came across the files containing my sermons I took a respite from my arduous undertaking. I was intrigued by what I had written and preached in my early years of ministry. Some old sermons I merely scanned; others I read word for word.   What a revelation! I found some interesting insights into myself and also into the spirit of the times three and four decades ago. I ended my safari into the past with two distinct feelings.

On the one hand, I felt a sense of dismay. I couldn't believe some of the things I wrote and said. What dear saints of God these people must have been to listen to what seemed like drivel to me. If suffering leads to maturity then the congregations I served must have been filled with full-grown Christians. They must have outdone Job in patience. I felt a twinge of shame as I rummaged through the ghosts of the past.

On the other hand, I felt a sense of amazement. I couldn't believe some of the brilliant insights and applications I made. For a young man to be so profound and so prophetic was almost beyond belief. What a keen mind. What a sharp intellect. With preaching of that caliber no wonder people made great strides in their spiritual life. It was hard to believe that these messages came from the same person.

I realize I am still a mixed bag. There is still much in my life that is so mundane ... so trite ... so insipid. I can become engrossed by the trivial at times. Things that don't really matter can still fascinate me. But I also recognize that I have matured. I know that I have made a difference in the lives of people. I am convinced that I contribute to God's work on earth. What I do and say is significant. I am aware that having a "dual personality" is part of being human. I am certain you have found that out too.

The wonder of grace, of course, is that God uses "mixed bags" to accomplish his purpose in the world. He does his work both in and through our strengths and weaknesses. He isn't stymied in accomplishing his goals because of our ineptness. He isn't dependent on our brilliance to achieve his purpose. But at the same time he uses our gifts and talents to bring about what he desires. Who we are really matters.

Like the Apostle Paul we still live our lives in *"weakness"* (I Corinthians 2:3), but we also rejoice in the truth that *"the Lord has assigned to each a task"* (I Corinthians 3:5), and that we are truly *"his fellow workers"* (I Corinthians 3:9).

Direction

It was one of those scenes that parents of adult children secretly delight in. (I'll be honest, we openly delight in them.) If you belong to that fortunate genre you'll understand. Let me illustrate.

It was a typical sultry Michigan evening in July. The sun was out, and a warm front from the south, like a giant humidifier, filled the air with an oppressive, invisible mist. Gladys and I decided a walk would be in order. We wended our way through the streets of our neighborhood in the silence of contentment, occasionally remarking on the appearance of someone's lawn or flowers. Thirty minutes later, drawn by an irresistible magnet, we ended up at the home of Randy and Bonnie, our son and daughter-in-law.

They were loading their trailer in preparation for a week of camping. **De-ja vu!** It was a ritual Gladys and I had gone through for fifteen summers while raising our family. Their treks from house to trailer and back again seemed endless. Decisions . . . and more decisions. What to take; what not to take. Each item from their sorties into the house needed to be packed in just the right place . . . sleeping bags here . . . clothes there . . . rubber rafts here . . . balls and bats there. Beads of sweat formed on their foreheads as they finished the monumental task of arranging and rearranging and tightening down.

We watched the proceedings with a knowing chuckle on the inside. Been there done that. Now it was their turn. "Lots of work, isn't it? Randy," I offered as a brilliant fatherly insight. "You know," he said, looking up with a smile on his face, "when I was a kid I thought camping <u>just happened</u>."

Isn't that a part of becoming mature? Nothing that is enjoyable "just happens." A fine meal, a comforting sermon, a pair of clean socks, and a good book . . . all are there because someone has worked behind the scenes. A word of thanks is always in order to those who prepare things for us.

I am also struck by how God has worked unobtrusively to shape the direction of my life. I thank God for his loving preparation in such things as the sequence of my places of ministry, the people he has brought into my life; and the daily delights I experience. Nothing "just happens." God is always at work. He *"neither slumbers nor sleeps"* (Psalm 121:4). He works even while I am not aware of it. I am certain you can say the same. Praise God!

Connections

*"**H**e's got connections!"*

The words exploded from his mouth like a fourth of July firecracker. They screamed of frustration, disappointment, and hurt. He was a young man in his late twenties. We had just finished a strenuous softball game at a group picnic and now we were standing in the shade of a gnarled oak tree sipping Diet Pepsi. I hadn't seen him for some time so in the course of our conversation asked him how work was going. I struck a nerve - big time! The bomb exploded! The cork was pulled! The dam burst! We slipped away from the crowd and sat opposite each other at a picnic table as he told me the story.

He had started working at the store part time while in high school and college. Soon after graduation he came on full time. It was a "marriage made in heaven." He enjoyed the people contact. He could practice his educational skills and express his artistic gifts. He climbed the proverbial ladder - foreman . . . department head . . . assistant manager. He waited patiently for the big one - store manager! Finally the opportunity dawned. The manager moved to another chain. My friend was the natural choice as replacement. Then the bomb dropped. He was passed over.

His emotions gradually surfaced as he talked. When he described the person who had been chosen he became especially animated. I interjected a natural question - why? That's when I got the sneering reply, ***"He's got connections!"***

I knew what he meant. The cliché is often true, "It's not what you know, but who you know." Sad to say, corruption in politics, injustice in business, and disappointment in church work are often the result of "connections." The right ties can supersede merit and competence.

Later, as I reflected on our conversation it occurred to me that not all connections are bad. I began to realize how God "connected" me with people who helped me become what I am today. I count numerous family members, teachers, and friends to whom I am connected whose gifts, love and presence have enriched my life. I thank God for those "connections." On many occasions each has been the *"friend who loves at all times"* (Proverbs 17:17).

I invite you to take a moment and consider the people God has brought into your life . . . people who have assisted, encouraged, and blessed you. It is usually the right person in the right place at the right time. I am certain you too can praise God for many of His "connections" in your life.

Tradition

A meal of broiled meat-spread buns, a green Jell-O salad, and a Danish pastry puff has become a significant entree in our family's diet over the past 54 years. I venture to say it has become a part of the DNA of the Draayer clan.

After our move to Philadelphia in 1958 Gladys and I and the three children celebrated Christmas away from our larger family for the first time. As a prelude to opening our gifts on Christmas Eve Gladys prepared the buns, the salad, and the pastry as a light snack. The children ate it with contentment, and then we headed off to the main event.

The next Yuletide it was the same script – buns, salad, and pastry and then the gifts. We slipped into the same pattern in the following years. The die was cast.

Some things changed in subsequent celebrations. Our family grew with the addition of Ken and Randy. We moved to various cities. On a few occasions parents or friends joined the seven of us. But there was one constant – the buns, the salad, and the pastry.

We realized how deeply entrenched this ritual was in our family psyche when our sons married. As our daughters-in-law eased into the annual rite they graciously offered to bring some food for the meal. Our boys were taken aback. To bring "foreign" food was almost sacrilege. Things had to be exactly the same. It was a time-honored tradition!

Traditions are a constant in an ever-changing world. They are the strong threads that run through the fabric of life and hold it together. They remind us that life is not a series of disjointed events, but is like a seamless cloth with a pattern that gradually becomes evident. Progress and change are inevitable and needful, but that can often leave us confused and anxious. Traditions give us the balance that answers the heart's need for continuity.

Continuity is at the core of Christmas. When we celebrate we rejoice that Christ's birth fulfilled God's promises of the past and assures his promises for the present and the future. As the carol puts it, "The hopes and fears of all the years are met in Thee tonight." God's work of salvation is the one great constant in the history of the world.

May your celebrations and traditions be a powerful reminder of God's continued presence in your work ... in your lives ... and in the world. To top it off – someday we will know fully his promise, *"I am making everything new!"* (Revelation 21:5).

Trust

My ministry as pastor of our church in Ann Arbor, MI, a university town, was a stimulating time in my life. It was a lively church with a good mixture of "town and gown" people. Our children were all happy in school and had good friends. It was an exciting city to live in. I was active in various ministries. I felt useful and fulfilled.

After five years I accepted a position as director of a servicemen's center. It was not an easy family move. Two months after arriving I realized the work was not for me. Six months later a church invited me to be their pastor. It was a 'no-brainer.' I accepted it.

The year in San Diego has been an unexplained parenthesis in my life. I've often questioned my decision. Why did I leave a vibrant ministry? Why did I disrupt our family life? I had no explanation. At times my only defense was 'temporary insanity.'

I still don't know the full reason for my *faux pas*. However, as I shared my thoughts with various people,

God gave me a new perspective on my brief hiatus from parish ministry.

David Rottenburg, who succeeded me as director, was laid off from his job as an engineer when I arrived and was unemployed for a year. He related to me that God needed my year there to prepare him for his new position.

Our daughter, Jan, who was most affected by the relocation, reminded me that she met her husband, Gil, at the Center. Our move provided the occasion for them to meet.

Our son, Ken, explained that watching servicemen at the Center work on their cars eventually led him into the auto body repair business. When Sherrie, now his wife, came in to have her car repaired, it was the beginning of their relationship.

All three saw clearly how God used the move to affect their lives in a mighty way.

I realize now that God used my poor judgment and 'insanity' for the good of others. He did not force me to make the move. I was responsible for that. But he worked in and through it to bless Dave, Jan and Gil, and Ken and Sherrie. That's the way God often works. He can take our mistakes . . . our failures . . . our blunders . . . our poor decisions and turn them into something good. He indeed is *the God of all grace*" (I Peter 5:10).

But even more, I have also been reminded of my own inadequacies and my need to trust in him completely. I have experienced again the truth that in Christ when *"I am weak, then I am strong"* (*II* Corinthians 12:10). I trust you have experienced that too.

For Our Good

Our daughter Jan surprised me on Father's Day with a large watercolor painting of the neighborhood grocery store our family owned in the 40's and 50's. A big part of my life revolved around that building since I both worked and lived there from ages 8 through 24.

It didn't take long after unwrapping the picture for nostalgia to kick in. I've reflected a lot on:

- The interactions with a wide variety of customers (mostly nice) on a daily basis;
- The Saturday afternoons which dragged because I had to work while my friends were playing ball (Incidentally, it's the best illustration of eternity I've ever encountered);
- The delightful hours I was able to spend working with my father;
- The many 'baseball' games my brother and I played in the aisles with a wad of paper and a yardstick when my dad was gone and we had no customers;

- Ration points for scarce items such as meat, coffee, and sugar during World War II;
- The feeling at times of being trapped because other work looked more inviting;
- Giving up ownership of the store when I had the call to ministry.

The business was the result of an extremely difficult event that altered our family's life forever. At age 36, my father was struck by a car while walking to his factory job. An improper diagnosis of his skull fracture resulted in three years of hospitals, pain, and poverty. Although doctors doubted he would ever work again he started selling groceries just for something to do. While he never fully recovered from the accident we did enjoy a modest livelihood from the store.

The predominant thought as I look back, however, is that God was working in and through this tragedy for our good. While working in the store my two sisters, my brother, and I learned to meet people, to understand them, and to serve them. It was a vital part of our education since we all ended up in people-oriented professions - one sister as a nurse, one in business, my brother in teaching, and I in the ministry. What we didn't see then became clear later.

Pain and difficult times are often unwelcome guests in our lives. We can end up anxious . . . frustrated . . . full of questions. But there is always more to the picture. God is at work. He has a way of taking those painful experiences and using them for our good. We may not realize it at the time, but slowly and surely we find that *"God works in all things for our good"* (Romans 8:28).

Partners

I've had the luxury many years of not having to cut my own lawn. Our grandsons, David, Nate, and Jonathan have been doing it all. It gives them the opportunity to make a few dollars while I sit in the shade, supervise, and sip a cold drink.

One Saturday while Nate mowed the grass I decided to pull up some of the unsightly weeds that seem to multiply like rabbits in our front yard. Jonathan, who was 3 at the time, eagerly assisted me. By the time we finished, the sidewalk was strewn with a sundry assortment of weeds and clippings.

I got out the leaf blower to push the debris along the walk to one point where I could sweep it up. My trusty assistant, Jonathan, decided that would be a good job for him. So, I handed the blower over to him. Then things got interesting. The thrust and weight of the blower made it a little difficult to control. But he was determined to do the job. So, while some of the sweepings went down the sidewalk as planned, some of it also went back on the lawn.

Decision time! Do I take over and do the job right? Or . . . do I let Jonathan finish his labor of love and I clean up a few things later? My grandfather instincts kicked in a nanosecond. A no brainer! Of course, he has to finish the job. It may not be the greatest, but his determination and desire to please me touched my heart. What else could I ask for?

I picture that as the way God relates to us. He allows us to be partners with him even though we don't always do a perfect job. You know how it is. We try to say something, but it just doesn't come out right . . . we forget a birthday . . . trivial things that waste our time . . . words we wish we could take back . . . opportunities for helping others that we missed. We don't prepare well to teach a lesson. Many times we do well, but we sometime leave a little mess behind. And he has to tidy up after us.

But he never loses his love for us. He accepts and uses what we do. As we offer up our efforts and the events of the day he reaches down and sanctifies them. In a way far superior to grandparents and parents he delights in the work we do in his name. We don't have to work harder to impress him. That allows us to *"sleep in peace"* (Psalm 4:8) and to wake up in the morning knowing that *"his compassions are new every morning"* (Lamentations 3: 22, 23).

Understanding

When I was about 10 a friend told me his uncle needed help in pulling up bean plants on his farm since the beans were all picked. We had a couple of days off from school that fall and the idea of earning some spending money sounded good. I readily accepted.

With some older boys we took a bus to the end of the bus line and his uncle picked us up in his truck and took us to the farm. We each were assigned a row of plants to pull up and place on a pile. For every row we picked we would get 50 cents – a princely sum in those days.

It was disaster from the word go. The ground was muddy from a previous night rain. The roots of the plants in the other rows went down about 6 inches; mine seemed to go down about 3 feet. The older boys worked faster and soon disappeared from sight. The end of my row stretched out *ad infinitum*. I was cold. By lunchtime I hadn't even finished a row and the older boys were starting on their third one. I needed to get out of there. But I also needed to save face. I didn't want to be seen as a softie.

I chose an age-old, non-arguable solution out of my predicament. I decided to have a stomachache. I told my friend why I had to leave. Then I walked the two miles back to the bus line and rode home. My parents graciously accepted my reason for coming home. My mother gave me some warm milk to drink and suggested I take a nap. When I woke up my dad gave me a few jobs to do in his store. It was a miracle! I was cured!

My parents, of course, saw through the scam I was trying to pull off. But they taught me a basic lesson in **understanding** Instead of chiding me, they entered into my situation as I constructed it and then gently led me out of it. No ridicule. No hard questions. They understood my embarrassment and gently nudged me in the right direction.

Isn't that exactly how God deals with us? Psalm 103:14 reminds us *"he knows how we are formed, he remembers we are dust."* He sees our foibles. He knows there are times we are overly anxious. He is cognizant of the times we make a mess of things. He is aware when we get discouraged. He sees through the masks we sometime wear.

And how does he respond? "... *the Lord has compassion on those who fear him*" (Psalm 103:13). With the gentleness of a parent he speaks an appropriate word. He sends a friend who does a kind deed. He assures us through the Christian community that we are his children. His goal is not to embarrass us or to tear us down. In his kindness he lifts us up and continues to use us in his service. What a great God we serve!

The Ordinary

I passed another marker on the road of life earlier this year – another birthday. The candles and the family celebration reminded me that, along with everyone, am not immortal. I was reminded, to borrow the title of Billy Graham's new book, that I am "Nearing Home."

Yet it was a great day. As the final seconds ticked away I felt a deep sense of well-being and fulfillment. I asked myself why. On the surface it was an ordinary birthday. Nothing spectacular . . . nothing earthshaking. Nothing, as they say, to write home about.

Then I began to realize it was the ordinary that made it extraordinary. It began with a hug and kiss from Gladys. A friend I met in the grocery store somehow remembered. Welcomed phone calls interrupted my day. Our sons called - Tom from Denver . . . Randy called during his break at school, as did Ron a few moments later. A stack of cards awaited me when I got home.

In the evening my 'same-day birthday' grandson, Nate, and I blew out candles together, posed for pictures, enjoyed ice cream and cake, and opened presents. Then, the phone again. Our daughter, Jan, and Gil from Alabama . . . my sisters from Grand Rapids . . . grandchildren in Denver and Alabama. I went to bed that night with a deep feeling of 'shalom.' What more could I ask?

What made the day special? The activities themselves were quite conventional. Probably no different than many of your birthdays. Ah, I know what it was. The kind words and gifts and hugs and kisses were an affirmation. They told me I mattered. I was special.

All the little touches . . . the commonplace . . . the 'normal' . . . added up to one big message of love.

But it went even deeper. Through their tender touches I also felt God's love and care. He spoke through their words . . . hugged me through their hugs . . . loved me through their love. That's a great truth to remember. We some time think God is only in the spectacular, the miraculous, the unusual. We like 'signs and wonders.' We like dazzling displays of God's dynamic power.

If that's our main focus we may miss him in the ordinary. So often he comes in the disguise of the common. He is the God who frequently speaks in the *"silent whisper"* (I Kings 19:12). My prayer is that you may be continually open to God's presence in the ordinary. And then, pass it on.

Delays

Delays usually are not pleasant. They irritate us. They waste our time. They upset our routine. Deliveries are late. People miss deadlines. The check doesn't arrive. Traffic is stopped. We get agitated. Our outlook sours. Frustration and anger settle in.

We ran the gamut of emotions in a delay one October at Amsterdam's Schiphol airport after arriving from Bucharest, Romania Our 10:45 a.m. departure to Detroit was delayed 15 minutes due to a minor repair in the PA system. No big deal. We waited, boarded, and tried to get comfortable in our seats.

We learned a new definition of minor, however. There would be another delay, but the problem was almost fixed we were assured. Whoops. Another delay. An hour elapsed. Another promise. Another delay. Two hours. The pattern continued. Promise. Delay. Restlessness and aggravation settled in. Four hours. We're ready. There's hope. Wait! We're not quite ready. We did quite well in keeping our composure. Five hours. The sides of the plane seemed to close in. The seats were getting harder. Our stomachs cried out for food. How much longer?

At six hours, a sortie inside the gate to grab a sandwich was interrupted by an announcement that we were ready to go. Yes! Let's go! No way. Yup, a delay. Seven hours. Amid some angry voices Gladys and I were fairly calm. After eight hours on the ground we were airborne. An eight-hour flight lay ahead. Sixteen hours in a giant steel cage! Whew! We were glad to be home.

Delays are upsetting and draining. They seem magnified when it appears that God delays. Prayers are not answered. Healing doesn't happen. Results of our hard work are slow in coming. Ecclesiastical machinery creeps while we wait. Why, we wonder, doesn't God hurry?

Christmas is God's reminder that with him there are no delays. His timetable is perfect. The birth of Christ occurred when *"the time had fully come"* (Galatians 4:4). Not a minute early; not a minute late. God knew the opportune moment. He knows it for the world. He knows it for us.

The celebration of the birth of Jesus is a good time to remember that, as the hymn says, God "does just what he says . . . in his time." May that be the source of your joy when you celebrate Christmas.

Character

Spring means the beginning of baseball season and that reminds me of the many, many games I played and watched. I played on the school teams through ninth grade. As boys we got together almost every summer night on the vacant lot across the street to play ball. I'll admit, I never was a star. If a trophy were given out for a mediocre player I would have been a strong candidate. But I always have enjoyed playing the game.

One game came to my mind recently. I was playing slow pitch softball in what was kindly called the "Over 40 League." Most of us looked back on 40 by quite a few years. We were an assortment of shapes and sizes and a wide variety of talent. We played to win, but with an exception or two most of us were in it for the fun.

In this particular game I was catching for our team, so I got to see the opposing players close up when they came to bat. The other team had a player who might have been a twin to Zaccheus – not in age, but in size. I'll call him Hal. He was a good player, but his lack of stature was quite noticeable. Each time Hal came to bat some of my teammates made some references to the fact that he was vertically challenged. It was all done in fun, I suppose, but it occurred every time he batted. As it happened, Hal worked with our son, Randy. The day after the game he talked with Randy about the game. He mentioned that he had taken a lot of razzing from our team. Obviously he felt some hurt, even though it was meant in fun. Then he said to Randy, "I suppose your dad was one of them too." Randy's instant response was, "My dad wouldn't do that." He was right. I hadn't.

In addition to the gratitude I felt that Randy knew his dad well, I was struck by another thing. Not only do we influence people by what we **do**; we also influence them by who we **are**. Being, as we often say, is as important as doing. Character counts.

In our busyness it's easy to forget that. We plan programs. We attend meetings. We set goals. We keep statistics. We cram calendars. As good as all these activities are the need for personal growth and strength can easily get lost in the shuffle.

God is also interested in who we **are** as well as in what we do. He is working in us as well as through us. He wants us to *"grow in grace."* (II Peter 3:18) He wants us to become more Christ-like. (Galatians 4:19). It is vital that we take time to cultivate our relationship with God. Unless we do our words will soon become hollow and our deeds will be a mere charade. When we do God will also use us effectively. How wonderful also to know that the Lord *"longs to be gracious to us"* (Isaiah 30:18)

Changes

I learned long ago that things often can happen even though it seems that nothing is happening.

When I was almost finished with seminary, Gladys' parents graciously offered to buy me a "preaching suit" as a graduation present. So in April I went to our local clothing store and found a beautiful dark suit with just a faint stripe in it - exactly right to wear in the pulpit. Since it was a wool suit we put it away for the summer. Upon ordination in the fall I would be ready.

I enjoyed a variety of activities that summer. No school. Time to play with the children. Softball on the seminary team. Some preaching. A classmate and I did a brisk business painting houses. It was a great break after the 5 1/2 years of schooling I put in since I left the grocery business.

In the fall we moved to Philadelphia where I was to be installed as pastor of Trinity Chapel. A few days before my first sermon I thought I should try on my new suit.

Whoa! Wrong suit? It didn't fit! The waist must have been measured for Goliath. Maybe it had stretched in storage.

But, the suit hadn't changed. I had. While scrambling up and down ladders all summer I had gradually lost 20 pounds! All without effort. Never thought about it. In the normal routine of the summer I had shed the excess weight which accumulated during my more sedentary, seminary life style. Fortunately, with the deft touch of a tailor's hand I was ready for Sunday.

It strikes me that life is often like that. We go about the things we are called to do . . . work . . . interaction with fellow workers . . . visiting . . . corresponding. Nothing spectacular. No unusual things seem to happen. We are just doing our tasks. And then we find out something did happen - a word we spoke mattered to someone . . . a smile encouraged another . . . a deed smoothed a person's life . . . a prayer gave an individual new hope. Things were happening without our knowledge.

In God's economy things also happen <u>within</u> us when we don't realize it. As we go about our daily tasks the

Holy Spirit is blessing and sanctifying and changing us. Quietly, often without our awareness, he *"transforms us into Christ's likeness"* (II Corinthians 3:18) as we live life on a daily basis,

What an encouragement to know as we do the ordinary that God is active in it.

Never Alone

What a difference a few words can make! I learned that in a vivid fashion several years ago.

It was a Saturday morning and I had to pick up some boxes of books from the office. The Waters Building was practically deserted as I wheeled my dolly up on the elevator to the third floor. I was back in a few moments with my load. When the door opened I pushed my cargo into the cage, said a cursory 'good morning' to the two people inside, and punched the button for the first floor. Two seconds later we were there. Alas! The door failed to open. I pushed the button several times. No results. I tried the "Door Open" button. Nothing! I pushed 2, 3, 4 and all the way to 7. Zilch. I tugged at the door. Nada. Everything was frozen. We were stuck!

Nervous? Scared? Panic? Not at all. But I found out strange things happen when you're stuck on an elevator. For one thing the elevator shrinks. What had been a 6 x 6 car now contracted to half that size. My fellow prisoners, who had been average size, now ballooned to 400 pounds each. A furnace kicked in and the heat became sauna-like. I began sweating profusely. My throat became as dry as the Sahara Desert. My legs started turning to Jell-O.

I reached for the emergency phone. It rang once . . . twice . . . three times. When a female voice answered I was ecstatic. "We're stuck," I blurted out. She told me help would arrive soon. But I <u>needed a word of assurance.</u> "You won't go away, will you?" I asked plaintively. "I'll be here," she said calmly. Great! Five minutes later we were set free from our temporary prison.

"I'll be here." That's what I needed to hear. Her words were words of assurance . . . assurance that we were not alone . . . that we were not abandoned . . . that help was coming.

Life can present us with similar situations. There are times we feel stuck . . . alone . . . maybe even abandoned. Every life has its own unique times of desperation. We feel isolated from people, and sometime even God seems to have forsaken us. We cry out, "You haven't gone away, have you, God?" Then we need his reassuring voice. We need his calm word saying He still cares.

How good it is to serve a God who is always with us. Even when we feel stuck and cut off, his voice comes through loud and clear. *"I have engraved you on the palms of my hands; your walls are ever before me* (Isaiah 49:16).

Beginnings

Paging through some old photo albums brought back warm memories of our camping days as a family. It was a delightful time of sitting around the campfire talking, laughing, and eating 's'mores . . . fishing from the bridge . . . meeting new people . . . floating on rafts propelled by gentle waves . . . relaxing on the beach . . . and enjoying God's magnificent creation. Even now our children reminisce fondly about those halcyon days.

We got into camping by default. Living on a pastor's salary with five children it was the only way we could afford to vacation. So in the summer of 1964 we made the plunge – we bought a 9'x18' tent . . . a camp stove . . . a lantern . . . sleeping bags . . . air mattresses. The works! We were raring to go.

Our first venture into camping was a catastrophe, to put it mildly. As greenhorns we were totally unprepared for some of the exigencies of camping. I hadn't learned to "trench" so our tent took in water like the Titanic during a rainstorm the first night . . . sand maneuvered its way into our sleeping bags, our clothes, and our food . . . four of the children took turns being ill on a daily basis . . . our shadeless campsite made the hot sun seem even hotter . . . primitive toilets added to our dismay. The two weeks seemed like an eternity. I was ready to give everything away!

When Gladys and I announced the next spring that we would not camp again our kids were appalled. They recited a long litany on the virtues about camping. Not to go again was unthinkable. Reluctantly we gave in. And we found our apprenticeship paid off! We made some adjustments and developed coping mechanisms. We not only began to enjoy camping, we looked forward to it. A few years later we bought a modest pop-up camper that became our summer home for the next dozen years. The aggravation of that first year has faded in comparison to the enjoyment we had since then.

Isn't that how God often works on a bigger scale? New beginnings can often be so difficult. You have gone through some of them, or perhaps are going through one right now. You move to a new locality . . . you begin a new job . . . you try a new hobby . . . you try to quit a bad habit . . . your family situation changes. And nothing seems to go right. You question yourself, and sometime question God.

And then God helps you work through it. He gives strength and endurance and guidance and hope. Gradually things begin to change. You learn to say with the Psalmist, "*My God turns my darkness into light*" (Psalm 18:28). Praise God for his wonderful provisions.

Laughter

I provided some good laughs for a group of people at one of our Paraklesis retreats . . . but not by choice.

The manager of the hotel where we held a retreat in Brazil graciously offered us all a boat ride to a nearby island off the shore of the Atlantic on our afternoon off. Our ship was an old time 100-foot wooden vessel with two masts and held all 45 of us easily. Powered by motor instead of sails it glided gracefully over the calm waters.

The hilly island was a beautiful, jungle-like mixture of trees and flowers. The brilliant shades of green sparkled in the bright sun. We were to be dropped off and hike 45 minutes to the other side where we would be picked up again.

Two ten-passenger dinghies brought us from shallow water to the ship and back to shore. It was while we were disembarking on the island that the spontaneous comedy began. I was the last to leave the dinghy. The timing was uncanny. No sooner had I put my feet in the water than a huge surge of seawater smashed into the small vessel, which then turned its wrath on me. In a trice I felt my feet falter . . . struggled a moment to regain my equilibrium . . . and then was dumped unceremoniously in 12 inches of salt water in a supine position. Shrugging off the indignity of my untimely spill I staggered ashore unhurt, but thoroughly drenched.

That's when the fun began . . . for others. I heard a chorus of hee-haws and snickers. And of course the verbal jests flowed freely. "That's the first time I've seen an underwater speaker." "I thought you could walk on water." "No lying down on the job." Our walk through the verdant terrain was also punctuated by occasional good-natured barbs hurled in my direction. To paraphrase a cliché, "A good laugh was had by all."

One of the greatest gifts God has given us is the ability to laugh. Laughter is rooted in God's grace. Laughter is filtering our incongruities and foibles through God's accepting love. It is reveling in God's goodness and undeserved favor even as we see our flaws and our feebleness. Life, of course, has its serious side. But when life is appropriately interspersed with laughter we are reminded that God is in control and that he loves us . . . warts and all. I pray there is room in your life for 'holy hilarity.' Remember, *A cheerful heart is good medicine* (Proverbs 17:22).

Choices

It was a pastoral call filled with emotions, and I ran the gamut . . . compassion . . . panic . . . confusion . . . a tinge of guilt . . . relief . . . and then once again, compassion.

Gladys and I were visiting in the home of a parishioner. Her hurts cut deeply. Her husband had walked out on her leaving her with four children. The older children blamed her for the breakdown of the marriage. Her job situation was insecure. We listened intently and caringly as she talked about her pain.

When she offered us coffee, we readily agreed. But along with the coffee came a generous slice of fruitcake. My insides screamed - No! No! No! Anything but fruitcake. Fruitcake is absolutely on the bottom of my list of foods. Negative adjectives flood my mind. My idea of eternal punishment is a diet of nothing but fruitcake. How could she do this to her caring pastor?

Now I faced a crisis. She had already suffered so much rejection. My pastoral heart said there was no way I could refuse her generous display of hospitality. But my body said "Don't you dare to eat it!!" Meanwhile, as I was writhing in internal pain, the slice had become 10 feet tall and weighed as much as the Empire State Building. How could I not hurt her and still escape bitter punishment?

One becomes very creative when survival is at stake. As we sipped our coffee I nonchalantly tore my napkin in half. Then, with a few well-orchestrated moves I gently nudged my nemesis into a piece of napkin. Timing, of course, is everything. At the opportune moment I thrust the paper-encased culprit under my sweater. Free at last!

The rest (pardon the pun) was a "piece of cake." With an occasional tug here and a push there I was able to work the nasty critter up to my shirt pocket where it sat calmly for the rest of our time together. With my body once more at rest I politely refused a second helping and was able to minister to her in a calm and caring way.

On the way home I offered Gladys a treat. She was shocked! She knew my dilemma and had been watching me like a hawk, but never detected my daring sleight of hand.

Life often presents us with difficult choices - choices much more serious than a fruitcake caper. To move or to stay . . . to confront or to back off . . . to speak or to be silent . . . to buy or not buy . . . to trust or not trust. Many times we need the wisdom of Solomon.

In those times of uncertainty we have a truth we can rely on. *"If any of you lacks wisdom, he should ask God, who gives generously to all without finding fault, and it will be given to him"* (James 1:5). We serve a God who cares about our decisions and has promised to guide us in those times when choices are difficult. In his time and in his way we will have the answer we seek. That is something we can be sure of.

Equips

We are nearing the end of grandchildren graduations from middle school, high school, and college as I write this. It's a festive time crammed with impressive ceremonies, fun-filled parties, and lots of reminiscence and projections. I wonder, given the flurry of activities and excitement, if anyone listens to graduation speakers. My most memorable graduation speech is the one I never gave.

As president of our gigantic class of 21 ninth graders my job, by tradition, was to give a brief speech at our graduation exercise. Our homeroom teacher would write the talk and I would deliver it. It was a simple task, but to us 14 and 15 year olds it was big time!

Alas, it never happened. After a few practice rounds my teacher decided I was not to be entrusted with such an awesome task. Too shy? Too quiet? Too nervous? She never said so directly, but I got the message. As an appeasement, I suppose, I was allowed to try out for the leading role in a brief play our class would present. Another rejection. I was relegated to the role of Bill

185

whose only lines were, "Martin? Is Martin home?" My one consolation is that even today people still tell me it was one of the most memorable lines ever uttered on the American stage.

How did I feel about it all? I suppose in some ways it was humiliation. One more step down and I would have been shut out completely. But, to be honest, I was relieved. I was talkative and at ease around my family and friends. But to get up in front of a group of people left me feeling shaky. I think I would rather have had four root canals than to stand before any crowd.

God must have chuckled at all this. Seven years later he whispered in the ear of this shy, quiet guy. And what did he say? "I have another spot for you." And where is that?" To the ministry where he would spend the next 54 years preaching and teaching. Who would have thought it?

Isn't that the way God often works? Moses couldn't speak, but God called him anyway. Paul was the greatest of sinners. God used him mightily. The truth is, when God calls, he also equips. When he puts us in a certain position, he also gives us the tools to do the job. Of course, we need to be certain of his calling. But when he calls, he is faithful.

When you struggle with a task for which you seem inadequate, or if a job looks too big, remember God often chooses the *"foolish"* and the *"weak"* and the *"lowly"* to carry on his purpose (I Corinthians 1:26-29). We don't need to make headlines. When we seek to do his will and are faithful to the task, he will give us what we need.

Criticism

I had to be careful how I sat a few days last summer . . . and all because a good deed backfired!

I was enjoying some yard work on a pleasant summer evening when a bee began buzzing around my head. It seemed to understand when I waved my arms that I didn't want its company and it flew off. A while later I noticed it had flown into the clear plastic bag into which I was tossing an assorted mess of thorns and thistles. Instinctively I closed the bag and watched my prey try to escape. I was ready to kill it, but then another scenario went through my mind. "This is one of God's beautiful creatures. It's only doing what bees do naturally. It's done no harm. Let it go." I listened, and away it went. I returned to my horticultural activity.

Five minutes later I felt a sharp pain on the back of my leg. A practical joker has poked a 12-inch needle into my leg, Not so! My "friend," the bee, to whom I had shown mercy . . . the one I had spared from certain death, had flown up into my shorts and skillfully placed its painful stinger high up on my leg. Ouch! With a couple of well-directed slaps I ended its earthly sojourn. But the damage had been done. As a result of its betrayal I was stuck with a painful red welt about four inches in diameter. Time did heal it.

In life we can sometime experience the same thing, but not from bees. People to whom we have we have opened ourselves up . . . to whom we have shown kindness . . . with whom we have worked closely . . . those we have counted as friends, can turn around and "sting" us. Their critical words and unkind deeds can hurt us to the very core of our being. We feel let down . . . disappointed. The betrayal of some leaves scars that take a long time to heal.

How do we respond? Often we'd like to strike back. We want to hurt them as much as they hurt us, even more sometime. But that's not God's way. *"Do not repay evil for evil,"* he reminds us in Romans 12:17. The key, I believe, is prayer and patience. We need to pray for the courage to act, if that is appropriate . . . for the humility to forgive . . . for the grace to keep loving . . . and for the will to stay focused.

And we need patience . . . patience to let the hurts heal . . . patience to get a true perspective . . . and above all, patience to let God direct the final outcome. After all, he's been on the receiving end of our "stings." He knows the hurts. Yet, for Christ's sake he loves us and forgives us. He can give us what we need to do likewise.

Refreshment

The bright July sun, the 102-degree temperature, and the dust swirling about our feet as we walked made it easy to go back in our imagination to a significant part of our country's history. Gladys, my brother Jerry, and I were walking the Oregon Trail. Nothing fake here. No transformation with Disney magic. No souvenir shops. This was authentic.

As we plodded through the arid territory Jerry, who is a history buff, filled us in on details about the trail. Winding its way mainly along the Platte, Snake, and Columbia Rivers the trail carried thousands of pioneers in the 1840s and 50s from Independence, MO to present day Vancouver, WA. Its 2,000 miles of wagon ruts stood in sharp contrast to our modern Interstate Highways. Indian attacks, cholera epidemics, grass fires, storms, and floods were among the many dangers. The beads of sweat on our foreheads and increasing thirst reminded us how people and animals alike faced fatigue and hunger in the barren country we were in.

We trudged along the forsaken trail discussing what life must have been like for them. And then . . . as we came over a ridge . . . we came upon a surprising sight! Spread out before us like a lush green carpet was a valley covered with hundreds of trees. It was from this exact spot that some of the first explorers in this area cried in delight, "Les Bois! Les Bois!" - French for "The woods! The woods!" (This is how Boise, ID got its name) Respite at last! The trees meant water, shade, protection, and supplies. What a refreshing sight! What a marvelous provision!

It is no wonder that God uses a tree as a symbol of his relationship to us. In Hosea 14:8 he tells us, *"I am like a* **green** *pine tree; your fruitfulness comes from me."* He speaks in that chapter of his forgiveness . . . his compassion . . . his healing . . . his love . . . and his nurture. All are the fruit of his grace. He richly supplies all that his people need.

When we celebrate the birth of Christ the Christmas tree stands out as a loving reminder of who God is and how he provides for us. What a blessing to know him as our God. And what a privilege to serve in his world in his name - the one who, like a green pine tree, fulfills all of our needs.

Congruence

Halloween always brings a fair share of gnomes, gremlins and elfins to our door for the usual trick-or-treat. Gladys and I enjoyed the colorful array of disguises and dress. All the munchkins get their treat, of course, and not a one fails to say thank you. It's fun.

Halloween was different for me as a kid. There was a gentle debate in our church family whether Halloween detracted from Reformation Day, the day when Martin Luther nailed the 95 theses to the church door. Since the two days coincided, some maintained to go door-to-door asking for treats downplayed the importance of the Protestant Reformation.

As a result we kids were what I now call either "thrilled, thankful, trick-or-treaters" or "reserved rigid, reformers." Our family fell into the latter category.

Even though we understood the logic of our parents, some of us still wondered what it was like on "the other side." My friend and I decided to find out. We would need masks, of course, to get a real feel for it. To raise money we collected newspapers from people in the neighborhood and then took them in a wagon to Standard Scrap Metal & Paper Co. The 10 cents we each got was enough for a mask and a piece of candy. A great start!

Alas! Our adventure into "sin" was short lived. As we walked down the alley trying to avoid detection, my heart sank. Coming toward us was my father! He said nothing, but simply held out his hand. With both shame and reluctance I handed over the mask. Rats!

I realized later my father wasn't trying to spoil our fun. He was being <u>congruent</u>. What he believed on the inside came to expression on the outside. His action was not based on a whim, but on conviction. His faith was alive and he applied it to all he did.

Integrating faith into everyday life is not always easy. We can quickly become "professional Christians." Our familiarity with spiritual and religious matters may blunt our awareness to the power and excitement of the gospel. We can become perfunctory in our prayers.

There are times we may do things because they are expected of us, even though our heart isn't in it.

That's why it's important to keep our own relationship to God vibrant. Jesus promised that *"the one who feeds on me will live because of me"* (John 6:57). Feeding on him may occur in prayer, meditation on Scripture, in nature, or in fellowship with other Christians. It is not so much <u>how</u> we do it, but <u>that</u> we do it. Keeping faith alive on the inside will enable us to keep it relevant on the outside.

God's Hand

Gladys and I, as all grandparents do, often reminisce about past experiences with our grandchildren. We delight in their accomplishments and chuckle at some of their antics. The memories are a great gift.

Recently we talked about an incident concerning our oldest granddaughter, Kellie. When Kellie was 4 years old our daughter, Jan, spent a few weeks with us along with Michael, age 2. Gil, our son-in-law, was in med school. Kellie and I frequently walked to the store to buy a few groceries or go for candy or ice cream. It was always a delightful time. I remember one day in particular. As usual, Kellie jabbered all the way as we strolled together. It was fun to hear her chatter about the many things that fill a four year old mind.

As we walked something caught my attention. About 7 or 8 houses down, a nondescript mutt on a leash was bluffing toughness by barking at passersby. I knew that Kellie was in a stage where she was afraid of dogs.

(Today she is an ardent dog lover). I wondered what she would do as we approached the yelping canine.

We came closer and closer. Five houses, then four, and then three. Would she notice? Sure enough, she did. But . . . as we approached the gnarling pup she never missed a beat. She kept on jabbering and then simply lifted her little hand . . . placed it squarely in mine . . . squeezed my hand more tightly as we passed her nemesis . . . and kept right on talking. Finally, when the yapping pooch was behind us she let her hand slip back to her side. The peril was over and she was safe.

What an analogy of how we relate to God. With the Psalmist all of us have times when "*dogs are <u>barking at us</u>.*" (Psalm 22:16). People seem to avoid us . . . we are disappointed by those we trusted . . . sickness lays us low . . . projects that seemed so promising end up in failure . . . financial difficulties take a disproportionate amount of our time and energy. We become fearful and begin to worry.

At such a time we can raise our hand and put it in the hand of our loving father. *"Your right hand upholds me"*

(Psalm 63:8). He will walk with us through whatever we are experiencing. People may not change and situations may not change, but we know he will sustain and protect us because our hand is in his.

Enjoyment

Our son, Ken, his wife, Sherrie, and Alex, 2 1/2, came for a visit one-summer evening a number of years ago. We did the usual . . . talked . . . had some cold drinks . . . watched Alex play with the toys. When he became restless, I offered to take him for a walk. Little did I know what I was to learn.

In front of the neighbor's house I looked back to see Alex on all fours on the sidewalk. I joined him as we watched with fascination some industrious ants scurrying in and out of their little hole in the crack of the sidewalk carrying bundles completely out of proportion to their body size.

We moved on. A few doors down, Teddy, a golden retriever, got our attention. We inched up the driveway, making sure Teddy was tied up. Teddy and Alex talked some dog language and Alex patted him a few times. Teddy loved the attention and he and Alex were reluctant to separate.

As we walked Alex said, "Listen." I heard nothing. Then, sure enough, a plane appeared on the horizon. We watched the magnificent, mechanical bird gracefully glide over our heads and then disappear leaving only a thin wisp of vapor. A few houses down some squirrels played tag (or whatever squirrels play) on a telephone wire. I stooped next to Alex as we watched the furry rodents scamper to and fro with evidently no fear of failing off their precarious perch.

Around a corner we came on an oscillating sprinkler distributing welcome drops of water to a parched lawn. With perfect timing we dashed past it without getting wet. But wait! That's not what sprinklers are for. So, it was back and forth a couple of times. We laughed as the cool water splashed our faces and dampened our clothes. We completed the walk as Alex filled his fat fist full of dandelions, which he carried home as a loving bouquet to his mother.

Wow! A five-minute adult walk had turned into a forty-five minute peek into the wonders of God's creation. In leisurely fashion I had experienced God's world through the eyes of a child. Alex helped me to see things that were there all the time. I simply hadn't taken the time to notice them.

God continually surrounds us with his gifts . . . nature . . . relationships . . . books . . . animals . . and many more – *"all for our enjoyment"* (I Timothy 6:17). The danger is our busy schedules and fast paced living can keep us from enjoying what lies within our reach. An old song reminds us "the best things in life are free." Take time to enjoy God's world. Nothing is more delightful.

Presence

Gladys and I spent eight exciting days in India in 2000 where I spoke to the staff of Mission India. The interaction with people, the distinctive food, the striking sights, and witnessing the rapid growth of the church made this a most memorable trip. One point of intrigue for me was city and freeway traffic.

Stops for traffic lights can best be described as "organized chaos." There were usually no discernible lines as automobiles, bikes, trucks, and occasional oxen vied to be as close to the front as possible. Leaving an extra inch or two of empty space seemed like a mortal sin. Brave pedestrians weaved their way through the jumbled mess with great expertise. Rowant, our hired driver's calm demeanor gave us a sense of assurance as we observed what must be a common ritual, but I must admit that we were happy to reach our destinations.

It was not only the sights that caught my attention, however, but also the sounds. At the traffic lights, car and truck horns joined in a continual chorus of dissonance. On the freeway, Rowant blew his horn every time we passed someone; they did so when they passed us. The sign on the back of almost every truck, "Please blow horn", also took me aback. What gives?

As I mused on the absurdity of it all I began to realize the horns were primarily a courtesy signal. Unlike the US where horns generally indicate anger or impatience, in India they often have a kinder message. They seemed to say, "I want to let you know I am here. This is my way of letting you know where I am." Now the invitation on the trucks made sense.

Gentle reminders of someone's presence and caring are always welcome. A whispered 'I love you' does wonders for the soul. An unexpected phone call lifts our spirits. A brief note lets us know someone is thinking of us. A kind deed is a friend's way of letting us know he/she is there. An invitation to visit tells us we are not forgotten.

God also has a way of letting us know he is here. *"He has not left himself without testimony"* (Acts 14:17). He gently reminds us of his presence through the change of seasons . . . the birth of a child . . . an unexpected check . . . and the smile of a friend. The message of his continual

204

company may come to us through a beautiful sunset . . . through a friend's promise of prayer . . . or through words of appreciation from someone we have helped. Like the disciples on the road to Emmaus, when our eyes and ears are open, we will recognize him in the many ways in which he makes himself known.

Forgiveness

It looked like an ordinary flashlight. But to me, age eleven, it was special. We were just coming out of the Great Depression, my dad hadn't worked for five years due to an accident, and World War II was in full swing. I had few things I could call my own. The flashlight was a prized possession.

I could do so much with it . . . real and imaginary. I could find my way around our dark basement. In bed, under my blankets, its soft beam allowed me to read the whole series of Dick Prescott's adventures at West Point. What's more, if the enemy invaded I could signal US troops or spot spies crawling around in the dark. I valued it almost as much as my baseball glove.

But there is, as Paul Harvey used to say, 'the rest of the story.' A few months after getting the flashlight I was summoned to the principal's office. There stood a policeman. He must have been 10 feet tall, with 3 or 4 assault weapons dangling from his belt. He gave his name and then asked if I had a flashlight. The gig was up! I had confused "mine with thine." Yes, I had stolen

206

the flashlight from Arlan's store. One of my classmates had been on an extended stealing spree and got caught. He named me as a partner on this one occasion. In a faltering voice I admitted my sin and told him the flashlight was under my pillow. He told me he'd go to our house and retrieve it.

I made the walk home, to use St. Paul's words, "with fear and trembling." My parents were sitting at the table drinking tea when I entered the kitchen. "We know about the flashlight," my dad said softly. I had only one question on my mind. "**Do you still love me?**" There was no hesitation. "Of course," they said, almost in unison. Their hugs underscored their words. I was overwhelmed. I put my head on the table and sobbed and sobbed. I had been forgiven! I was accepted! No words could have been sweeter. No words had more meaning. Forgiven! A priceless gift!

What awesome power forgiveness is. <u>Hearing</u> it releases . . . heals . . . affirms . . . transforms . . . and brings life. <u>Speaking</u> it to others does the same. In our busyness it's easy to overlook someone who desperately needs the cleansing power of forgiveness. I continually pray that I will never miss an opportunity to pass on to others what I have received.

How good also to know that when we fail God and we reach out to him that *"He is faithful and just to forgive us our sins"* (I John 1:9).

Stability

I couldn't believe I missed the whole thing! Went completely by it. 'Twasn't the proverbial needle in the haystack or a pair of socks in the drawer. It was an entire city. Not a country cross road. Not a village. It was Cologne, Germany. Population 1,008,700. Drove right by it!

In 1989 Gladys and I took a self-guided 17-day vacation in Europe. We flew from Detroit to Amsterdam overnight, landing there late morning. We planned to drive an hour or so before finding a hotel. But a brief nap alongside the road revived us and we decided to go on to Cologne. Checking a map, I "knew" we had to take the autobahn to route 3 into town. What I didn't realize was that it was route 3 <u>in</u> town, but another number outside of town. So we drove, and drove some more. We saw a few signs to the city, but not route 3. Then . . . no more signs for Cologne. I checked the map. We had gone completely by it! And I wasn't sure where we were.

What you need to understand is that I'm not talking about an ordinary tourist. I consider myself a connoisseur of maps. I read maps for pleasure. I collect maps. Maps stay in my head the way Greek and Hebrew never did. Throwing a map away is almost tantamount to throwing a Bible away. So, here we were in this lovely wooded countryside in a foreign country not sure where we are. With jet lag setting in, my brain was now functioning with the proficiency of a bowl of oatmeal.

Then my homing pigeon instincts kicked in. We drove in what I thought was the right direction. After 15 plus kilometers and a few turns . . . jackpot! Through a clearing in the trees, like a giant guardian of the city, loomed the famous 740-year-old Cologne cathedral! The Dom! Awesome! With its 515 feet-high twin spires serving as a reference point the rest was a piece of cake. Within an hour we were in our hotel room in the shadow of the cathedral overlooking the Rhine River.

In the perilous journey, which we call life, God also gives us fixed points of reference . . . stability amid change . . . surety in uncertainty . . . encouragement in anxiety. Sometime a passage of Scripture becomes that unmovable point . . . or words of a friend . . . a specific answer to prayer . . . or the birth of a child. All remind us that God is still in control and that He continues to love us. God *"does not change"* (Malachi 3:6). He fills our lives with markers of the reality of his presence. We need only keep our eyes open to their existence.

And then to think that God can also use our words and deeds as a point of reference to others. What a privilege we have as Christians. We need to pray that we will be faithful to the task.

Trustworthy

On our trip to Denver a decade ago Brad and Leanne, our grandchildren, kept asking me to let them drive the car even though they are under age. What's a grandpa to do? I relented, much to their delight. It also reminded me of my early under-age driving experiences.

I frequently rode with my father on his weekly trek to my uncle's chicken farm to pick up eggs. "Farm-fresh" eggs were a big seller in our store. I have fond memories of our chats during the half hour rides into the country, the last mile or two on an unpaved road.

One day he stopped the car as we swung on to my uncle's road and asked me if I would like to drive. I was 11 years old at the time. Wow! Really? I was ecstatic! I jumped into the driver's seat, and after a few stalls trying to master a stick shift we were on our way. What a thrill. I deftly maneuvered around the ruts and proudly turned into the driveway. Three days later, as it seemed to me, we left and I again drove the unpaved road.

Driving became my passion. My weeks revolved around Thursdays, the day we usually went. Fantasies abounded. I was a B-19 pilot dropping bombs on Germany. I was a racecar driver taking the checkered flag at Indy. I skillfully weaved ambulances through traffic bringing an injured person to the hospital. I drove a fire truck with sirens blaring on the way to put out a massive conflagration. It didn't get much better than this.

Later he even let me drive a stretch on the paved road and do some restricted city driving, until I got my license at age 14. Even now I have not forgotten the joy of those early days.

What made it all so special? Of course, there was the thrill of driving. But there was more than that. My father gave me a gift – the gift of <u>trust</u>. When he allowed me to take the wheel he was basically saying, "You are a trustworthy person." He communicated in non-verbal fashion that he had confidence in me. He helped me learn to trust and be trusted. It was a fatherly gift . . . a gift that helped shape my life.

God has also given us the gift of trust. He *"entrusts us with the gospel"* (I Corinthians 4:1, 2). He entrusts us with the lives of family . . . friends . . . fellow Christians . . . the care of his earth . . . and bringing about his purpose in the world.

God's message through all this is that he finds us trustworthy . . . that he has confidence in us. That defines who we are. That is why we need to guard against defining ourselves by our busy schedules . . . our accomplishments . . . or our position. We can rest in the confidence that he trusts us. We are simply called to be faithful, and he will do the rest.

How wonderful to serve a God who himself is trustworthy. (Psalm 11:7)

Provision

The winter scene I saw is one of those that is hard to describe. Under the cover of darkness, while we slept, God had painted the rooftops, the trees, shrubs and lawns pure white. The cotton-like snow glistened in the bright sunlight. From the wide glass expanse of my third floor office I had an exceptional view of God's handiwork. The bitter cold only made the scene more vivid.

It was the trees just outside of my window that especially caught my attention. Right next to my window stood five tall, slender pines like sentries on duty, each with their long, green needles full of delicately shaped snowflakes. In the center court were trees with snow-covered branches raised to heaven like a white-robed choir of praise. And right below me is what I call "the berry tree," a tree with bright red berries almost all year around. On this cold morning the berries popped their heads through the snow looking like an army of red polka dots on a white sheet.

But the intriguing part was the birds. All day long . . . sometime solo, sometime in a group - they came to feast off the berries. What a variety! Cardinals with their bright red coats; finches with various shades and configurations of yellow; nondescript, gray sparrows; no-nonsense blue jays with their sharply manicured crests, and others I didn't recognize. All of them feeding off the goodness of God's creation on this clear, crisp winter day.

It was not only the beauty of God's creation that captivated me but also the awareness that in this day-long drama that I witnessed was a literal fulfillment of Jesus' words in Matthew 6:26, *"Look at the birds of the air; they do not sow or reap or store in barns, yet your heavenly Father feeds them."* And then he makes an application *"Are you not much more valuable than they?"* (vs. 27).

I need that reminder constantly. I am sure you do too. Worry so easily walks into our lives uninvited. Like Martha we become anxious about many things. How good it is to know that the father who feeds the birds also has promised to supply all of our needs. Even in the "winter of the soul" he is there with exactly the right thing. The birds are his reminder.

Interruptions

We were getting nowhere fast. Gladys and I were taking care of our three grandsons and agreed as a part of the pact to put them to bed. Their delaying tactics were superb. What one didn't think of, the other did. Finally, I decided it was time to throw a little psychology into the friendly battle of wits we were having. 'Let's see," I said with all the excitement I could muster, "who can get their pajamas on **first.**" Bingo! They bit! Now it was a **race**. What could have dragged on for hours was now measured in milliseconds. Different view; different response.

It was not, of course, a stroke of genius on my part. If you're a parent or grandparent or work with children you probably have done something like that on many occasions. (Until they get wise). A different point of view can mean a change of behavior or attitude. In counseling it is called 'reframing.' In my training we were taught to use this tool to open another window through which people could view their situation. A new look can give new hope, new energy, and new responses.

Gladys and I sometimes 'reframe' in our lighter moments. When we flew a lot with our work for Paraklesis we decided to get a credit card that gave us airline mile credit for every dollar we spend. So, when we make a purchase that produced just a tinge of guilt, one of us would say, "Think of it not as spending money, but as earning miles." The guilt melted as quickly as a snowflake in the April sun.

I believe there is a place for 'reframing' in the Christian life. Looking at a situation in a different light can give us a new perspective. One thing I am thinking of is interruptions. Interruptions have a bad reputation. Even the sound of the word can produce the shivers. (Something like the words 'root canal'). Interruptions often leave us frustrated and upset.

We can also view interruptions as **opportunities**. Not all of them, of course. I have little patience for the salesperson who calls at dinner time to sell me screen doors because "I just happen to be in your neighborhood." Yet, I have learned that most of my interruptions have been opportunities for me to respond to someone or something with a *"cup of cold water"* (Mark 9:41) in Christ's name.

I have also learned that many of life's major interruptions - illness, delays, and setbacks have been opportunities for me to experience God's grace in new ways. I pray that God who gives us uninterrupted access into his presence will also help you to reframe your interruptions.

Rest

I remember the first time I saw her. It was love at first sight. I had just graduated from high school. She was 13 years old, but I thought she was beautiful. Her body was solid and well taken care of. She could run with the best of them. I knew I'd be proud to be seen with her. I couldn't resist. So I bought my first car, a 1936 Ford.

It was a great car. I washed and waxed it regularly, serviced it on time, and usually drove with caution. My only problem with it came one night after dropping off a friend. As I was heading home I heard a persistent squeak coming from the rear of the car. I decided to ignore it, but the volume increased. I stopped the car to see if I could find the trouble. I saw nothing amiss. All the service stations were closed so I decided to keep going.

The crescendo, however, increased. I knew something ingenious had to be done. Then it came to me. I turned on the radio. Sure enough, the piercing cry went away . . . but not for long. The shrilling sound soon overcame the soothing music. I turned up the volume. Peace . . . but it was short-lived. The rear end begged for attention. I upped the volume. It counter moved. The silly game went on until I got home. Fortunately, no damage was done and a mechanic fixed the problem the next day.

My ploy, of course, did nothing to cure the cause of the cacophony. It was only a distraction whereby I tried to keep my mind off the real problem. I tried to trick myself into thinking nothing was awry. I knew I was wrong, but I kept it up anyway.

It's easy to use distractions to keep our minds off issues that need to be addressed. That is one of the hazards of Christian life. We need to be careful that our full schedules are not a way of avoiding unpleasant issues. Our crammed Smartphones may be a tribute to our importance, but they can also indicate something is really calling for our attention.

Being overly busy can be a cover up for feelings of inferiority . . . for grudges we harbor . . . or for a painful situation we wish would go away. Our absorption in activities can be a way of avoiding a broken relationship or a difficult task. There may be a bad habit we cannot shake. We may be speeding along, but we are dying on the inside.

How much better it is to admit the struggle we are having and open it up to others and to God.
Remember the words of Jesus. *"Come to me . . . and I will give you rest"* (*Matthew* 11:28). As he heals us from within, he frees us to enjoy him more fully, releases us from the captivity of the calendar, and allows us to carry out our life more effectively. Remember, he is the God who *"heals all our diseases"* (Psalm 103:3).

Joy

Occasionally Gladys and I will rent a movie when we both are in the mood for some entertainment. So one night some years ago I made the trek to the rental store to find something we would both like. It was slim picking. I was ready to go home in defeat when I spotted the new release of <u>The Count of Monte Cristo</u>, the classic book by Alexandre Dumas. So we made some popcorn, poured a cold drink, and sat back in our comfortable chairs to enjoy the movie.

In the movie Edmund Dantes, the main character, is betrayed by his enemies and thrown into a secret dungeon the Chateau d'lf . . . doomed to spend his life in a dank prison cell. Once a day some food is shoved under the door. Each year on the anniversary of his entrance he is severely whipped. He languishes for years in his dreary cell when one day he hears some tapping. Suddenly some tiles on his floor rise up and a fellow prisoner emerges. He had spent years digging a tunnel to escape, but had made a wrong turn.

Now they plot together to finish the tunnel and escape. For us, the suspense builds as they spend over a year painstakingly clawing and chiseling their way through dirt and rock. At last they are near their goal. Then, without warning, the tunnel collapses and his new friend is seriously injured. Edmund hauls his friend back to his cell and just as he leaves to go back to his own cell the guards come in. Surely they will be found out! Now the suspense reaches crescendo stage.

At this point Gladys was almost on the edge of her chair. "Will he escape?" she asked with an anxious voice. I calmly assured her he would. You see, <u>I had read the book.</u>

The question of outcome is one we all ask on occasion. Sometime it is about the world in general. The chaos, the hatred, and the immorality seem out of control. Where will it all end? Sometime we ask it about our own lives. Disappointments, hurt, severe illness, uncertainty and many other things trouble us. If only we knew how it will turn out.

Thank God for the message of Christmas. We can celebrate God's answer to our questions. <u>We have read the book</u>. We know the outcome! The coming of Jesus is God's first step in making all things new. Our world will one day be completely changed. And so will we! That is why our celebration is a celebration of joy.

And there is even more reason for joy. For we have been called by God to bring that message of joy to a world that wonders how it will all turn out. My prayer is that *"the joy of the Lord will be your strength"* (*Nehemiah* 8:10) and that you will pass it on to others.

Cared for

I loved it immediately! I was reluctant at first, but under gentle coaxing from Gladys I agreed to take a 'holiday' (as the locals say) in London prior to our March retreat in Belgium. I'm not sure why I resisted. London turned out to be one of my favorite cities. We returned at least 6 times.

I loved the activity. There were the ubiquitous black taxicabs and the lumbering double-decker buses (all driving on the "wrong" side of the road). There were people . . . tourists with cameras . . . serious, dark-suited business people, . . . hordes of people swallowed up by the underground system only to be disgorged a short time later at another location.

I loved the sights. We were in awe as we viewed Westminster Abbey and worshipped at St. Paul's Cathedral. We froze waiting to view the changing of the guard at Buckingham Palace. The Tower of London has its share of grisly and romantic history. We ate at Harrods and got a historical perspective on culture at the British Museum and on war at the Imperial War Museum. Mixing this in with two plays and ethnic restaurants made this a great 4 days.

I loved the walking. It was while walking that one detail caught my attention. At each cross walk, painted on the street just beyond the curb, in letters at least 12" high, were the words "LOOK RIGHT," and at the mid-street island "LOOK LEFT." What a timely, thoughtful reminder to all of us who are used to traffic coming from the other direction! I felt cared for.

It occurs to me that God often does that with us. In a world where "traffic" often comes "from the wrong direction," and we are tempted to walk into it, he gives us little reminders to "look right" or "look left" before we act. He wants to prevent hurts.

Sometime we overwork and our bodies become his messengers telling us to slow down. At other times he uses the tender advice of a friend to keep us from "stepping off the curb" when our behavior or attitudes are harmful. *"Wounds from a friend can be trusted"*

228

(Proverbs 26:7). Often he uses his Word to stop us short when moving ahead would be to our detriment.

In London I felt concern for my physical safety. How good it is to know we serve a God who cares about our total safety. *"Cast all your anxiety on him because he cares for you."*(I Peter 5:7).

Healing

Do you remember those ubiquitous ads that seemed to pop up every summer? "Christmas in July." It's a not so subtle attempt by those clever people on Madison Avenue to create a mood in our heads while dipping their fingers into our wallets. The first time I was personally approached was in a restaurant! From the continual yuletide music to the menu to the pseudo-sincere "Merry Christmas" of the waitress we were supposed to believe it was December and thereby, I suppose, spend more money and leave a bigger tip. It was obnoxious to say the least. It felt a little like wearing brown shoes with a black tuxedo. No, I didn't leave a bigger tip and we skipped dessert!

Yet, interestingly, Gladys and I have experienced Christmas in July (well, it was August, really). But this time it was God who showed us. Of all places, it was at Mount St. Helens. It was the volcano that exploded in 1984 and devastated 230 square miles of forest

We traveled to Mount St. Helens in the summer of 1994. Getting off I-5 South of Seattle we stopped at the museum. We looked at displays which gave a history of the mountain before and after and then viewed the film of the mountain blowing its stack. It was awesome! Nothing could resist its path of death, destruction, and devastation. We left the museum and rode toward the mountain in a reflective mood.

As we got closer to the mountain, however, we were amazed. Growing out of the waste, unaided by human hands, we saw colorful bushes, flourishing trees and a verdant landscape. Out of death had come life; out of ruin came richness. A miracle!

One evening, about a month later, when I came home from the office, Gladys told me what she read in her devotions that day. *"I will put in the desert the cedar and acacia, the myrtle and the olive. I will set pines in the wasteland, the fir and the cypress together, so that the people may see and know, may consider and understand, that the hand of the Lord has done this"* (Isaiah 41:19,20a). "That reminds me of Mount St. Helens," she said.

In our discussion we realized again that what God does in nature he also does in our lives. Slowly sometime, but surely, he rebuilds what is broken down, he fills what is empty, and he brings joy where there is despair.

Isn't that what Christmas is really all about? God invading our broken world with love and grace and life. Where human efforts have failed he has intervened with his power and healing. But Christmas is not just for December. Mount St. Helens is a constant reminder that it is for July and all the other months too.

What a blessing to know that the God who *"sets pines in the wasteland"* loves us in Jesus Christ.

Control

The pain, the frustration and the fear of my bout with Wegener's Granulomatosis in 1987 still creep vividly into awareness on occasion. As I mentioned earlier it's an auto-immune disease that was formerly fatal but now is treatable.

The month from the onset of my symptoms to a correct diagnosis was a time of nonstop uncertainty, hurt, and trepidation. I moved from specialist to lab to lab to specialist. I seemed spent more time in doctors' waiting rooms and cubicles than I did at home. Examining tables became as familiar to me as my own bed. I endured myriads of needle pricks and had dozens of snips of tissue extracted from my carcass. Almost every cavity in my body was searched I became a citizen of the world of white coats, x-rays, stethoscopes, and tubes of blood. I said many a prayer of thanks to God when I finally received the medicine to control my symptoms and start me on the road to recovery.

Once I started to feel better I went on a month-long cleaning binge. I vacuumed . . . I scrubbed . . I mopped.

No task was too menial. I declared war on cobwebs and dirt. Our cars glistened like new fall snow on a moonlit night. Weeds heard me coming and cowered in fear. I aligned anything that looked out of place. I cast a wary eye on anything that looked like junk. My children begged to come to their houses and continue my monumental crusade at their houses. Finally, to the delight of some and the chagrin of others, my fervor waned.

My medication caused some of the excessive energy behind my sanitary campaign. But there was a deeper reason. I wanted to bring order back to my life. For a month everything seemed out of control. Life had become a series of unmanageable events. I felt like a ping-pong ball being flung over the net in a championship game. I longed for equilibrium in my life. In the end, as I reflected on it all I began to realize that it was <u>God</u>, not I, who was really in control.

We all have occasions when life seems out of control. Illness strikes without warning . . . people we trusted blindside us for no apparent reason . . . our children engage in rebellious behavior . . . the bottom drops out of financial cache . . . our passion for work vanishes like kids at clean up time. We easily become discouraged . . . bewildered . . . undone.

As we struggle how good it is to know that even then God has his hand in our lives. He assures us he is still master of the storm . . . the tender shepherd . . . the rock of refuge. *"Do not be terrified; do not be discouraged, for the Lord your God will be with you wherever you go."* Joshua 1:9. Whatever the circumstances we can be certain he will see us through.

Decisions

Do you remember Michael Jordan? Experts agree he was probably one of the greatest basketball players of all time. I say it modestly, but he and I have some things in common.

Like Michael I've dazzled large crowds with a stunning array of in-your-face slam dunks . . . off balance game-winning three pointers . . . and a smooth-as-silk fakes that leaves defenders leaning like straw men in a strong breeze while I go in for another easy deuce. Alas . . . I do it in my dreams; Michael does it in real life. No comparison there!

What we do share, however, is that both of us announced our retirement at about the same time in 1993 . . . he from basketball and I as Director of Paraklesis Ministries. And then we both reneged at about the same time. Michael recanted after failing to connect with 90 mile-an-hour fastballs and deceptive change-ups in AA baseball. I retracted after further prayer and consideration.

Through further reflection on the process I am reminded of God's guidance and our decisions.

Some decisions have God's *imprimatur* on them from first thoughts to final execution. Doors open . . . affirmation abounds . . . all lights are green. We **know** they are of God. Other decisions we look back on with "how-could-I-have-done-that?" wonderment. We hang adjectives like 'mistaken,' 'stupid,' and 'crazy' on them. Good news! Even though they are, God still accomplishes His purpose.

Some decisions are not as easy to define. They seem so right. We start out and then we find God nudging us down a different path . . . unexpected . . . surprising . . . different . . . but always good. It's as though God says, "Be on your way and then I'll show you where to go." After Joseph decided to "*divorce Mary quietly*" God stepped in and redirected him. (Matthew 1)

How good it is to know as we make decisions that <u>God is always there.</u> Sometime his validation is readily apparent. At other times he works his purpose despite our "poor" decisions. And often his guidance becomes apparent only when we are on the way. Rather than becoming fearful or reckless in our decisions we can trust that as we commit our choices to him he will lead us and guide us in the right path. *"He will be our guide even to the end"* (Psalm 48:14).

Grace

I've been tempted to add to the simplistic "How To" books that seem to multiply like rabbits on the shelves of Christian Book Stores. Mine would be on marriage and entitled, "Ten Easy Steps to a Blissful, Painless, and Always Exciting Marriage." After all, I do have some credentials. Gladys and I celebrated 61 years of marriage in May, 2012.

I've decided, however, not to write the book. The truth is I couldn't think of even one or two easy steps, let alone ten. If I were to write a book I might entitle it, <u>It's All Grace.</u> As we look back on our three plus decades together we acknowledge that at each turn of the sometime rocky road of matrimony it was God's grace, and his grace alone, that sustained, encouraged, and led us.

We managed, with a good infusion of his grace, to adjust to the quirks and foibles we both brought to our union, and were able to open our hearts and lives to each other as we worked our way to greater intimacy and deeper trust.

With his help we learned, and are still learning, to reconnect after harsh words or careless deeds caused some distance.

He enriched our lives with five children, sixteen grandchildren and three great-grandchildren. Their affection and exuberance have been a continual source of joy and fulfillment for us.

He gave us wisdom as we raised our offspring, and graciously protected them from our failures and mistakes, and we felt his healing hand and caring presence during their illnesses.

We heard his voice in the encouragement of family and friends when I moved from selling pork chops and grinding hamburg to the college and seminary classrooms and on to ministry.

We were privileged to bring his love to people in four congregations, the Christian Counseling Center and Paraklesis Ministries. In turn, we experienced his love through them.

He embraced us with his love when Gladys suffered a major heart attack and let us cry in his arms when our son, Ken, died at age 45.

We experienced gentle eruptions of his beauty and power as we enjoyed majestic mountains, babbling brooks, surging seas, and delightful deserts in our worldwide travels.

He waved his arms in warning when we went down wrong paths, welcomed us with open arms when we sinned, and lifted us up when we felt discouraged.

He showed us how to laugh and how to take time to enjoy his world without feeling guilty.

He provided respite from busy schedules through family vacations, special times with just the two of us, and moments of worship in solitude and with his world-wide body.

I am reminded of John Newton's hymn, "'Tis grace that brought me safe thus far, and grace will lead me home." The words of Psalm 86:15 are so true.

He is *"a God of grace."*

.